VIRPAZAR ŽABLJAK STARI BAR CETINJE

40in14

A SCENT OF PODGORICA BUDVA

MONTENEGRO

Author
Paulo Cachim

Title
40 in 14 - a scent of Montenegro

Design
Paulo Cachim

ISBN:
9781530309115

40 in 14

A scent of Montenegro

Paulo Cachim

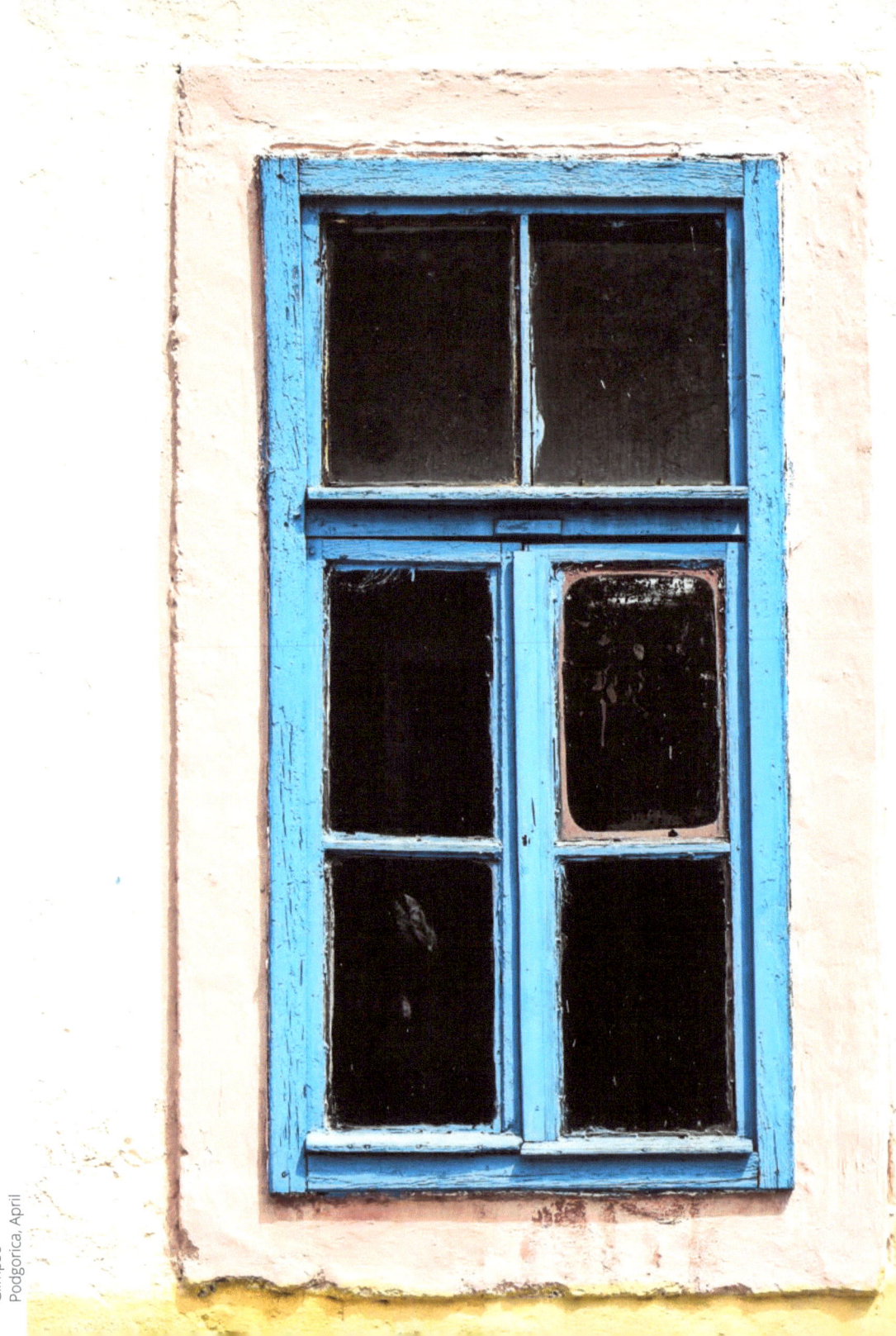

In 2014 I spent 40 days in Montenegro. The first time was in February and I went to Zabljak, the second time was around April-May and I stayed in Podgorica. Despite being a very small country, Montenegro has an incredible variety of landscapes. Mountains, beaches, canyons, lakes, fjord, there is always something for everyone. On the crossroads of empires, Montenegro offers an interesting mixture of cultures. A variety of architectural styles coexist from medieval times to today, throughout the Ottoman Empire, the Kingdom of Montenegro and the socialist period.

That year, the weather was really strange, or so I was told. When I arrived there for the first time, instead of snow, I found nice spring weather. It gave me the opportunity to walk in the proximities of Zabljak, a very rewarding experience.

The second time, in April-May, someone told me that this time of the year was really pleasant. Warm temperatures, sun, it was the best time of the year. That someone was wrong. It rained almost every day. Still, invariably grey and cloudy days can give rise to the most beautiful and improbable scenes. And sometimes after the rain, an incredible sun peeked out from behind the clouds, originating an amazing light.

Travelling around Montenegro by car, by bus, by train or simply on foot, offered me the opportunity to take a few hundreds of photos. Forty of those photos are displayed here. A scent of Montenegro. I hope it will be enough for you to put your feet on the road and taste some of the flavours of Montenegro.

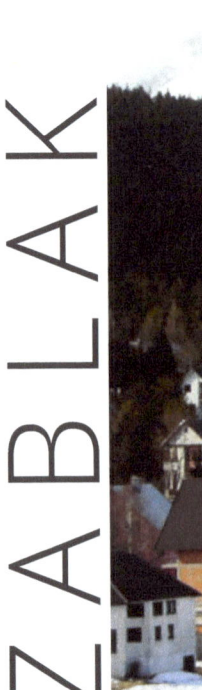

ZABLAK

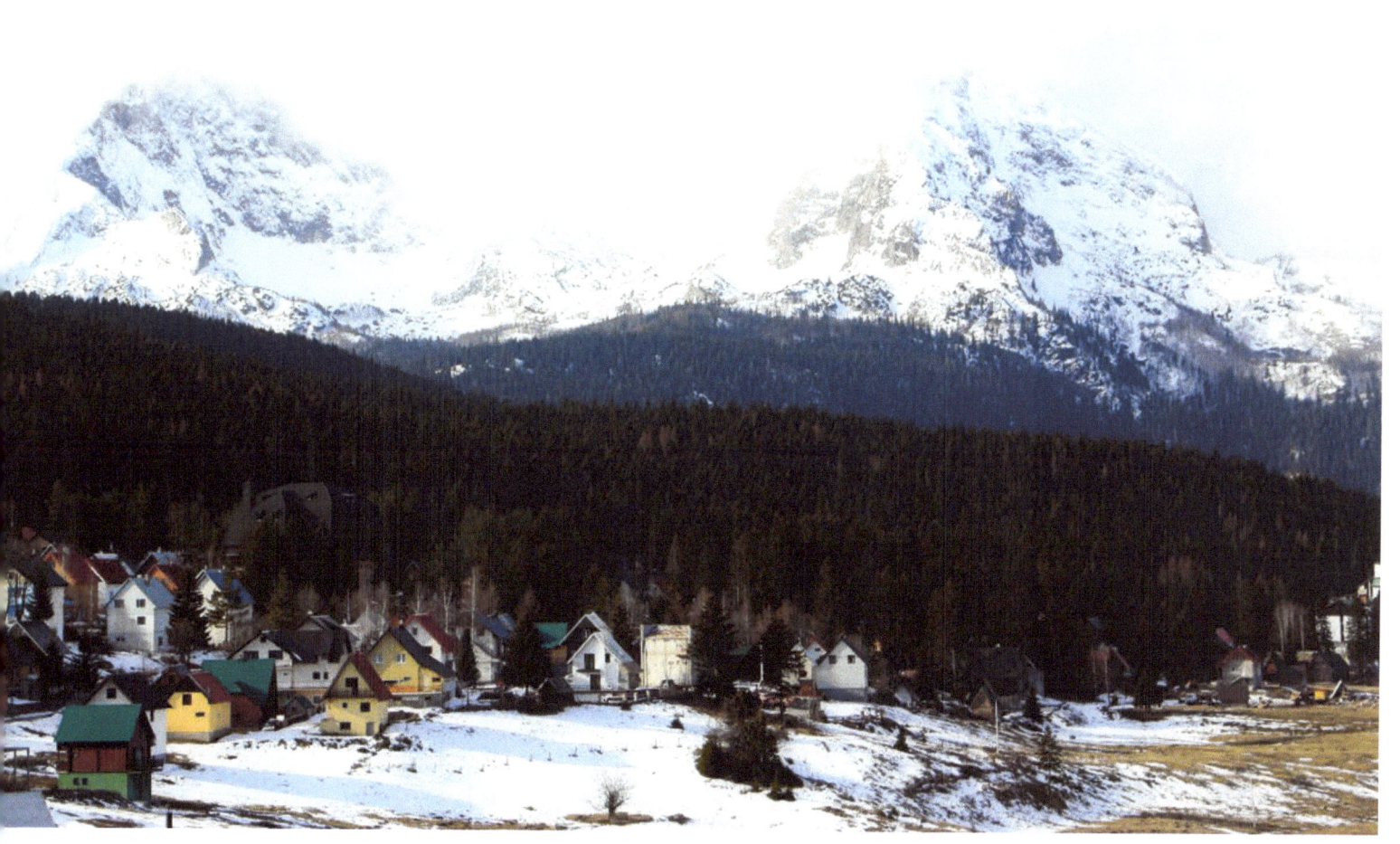

White
Zabljak, February

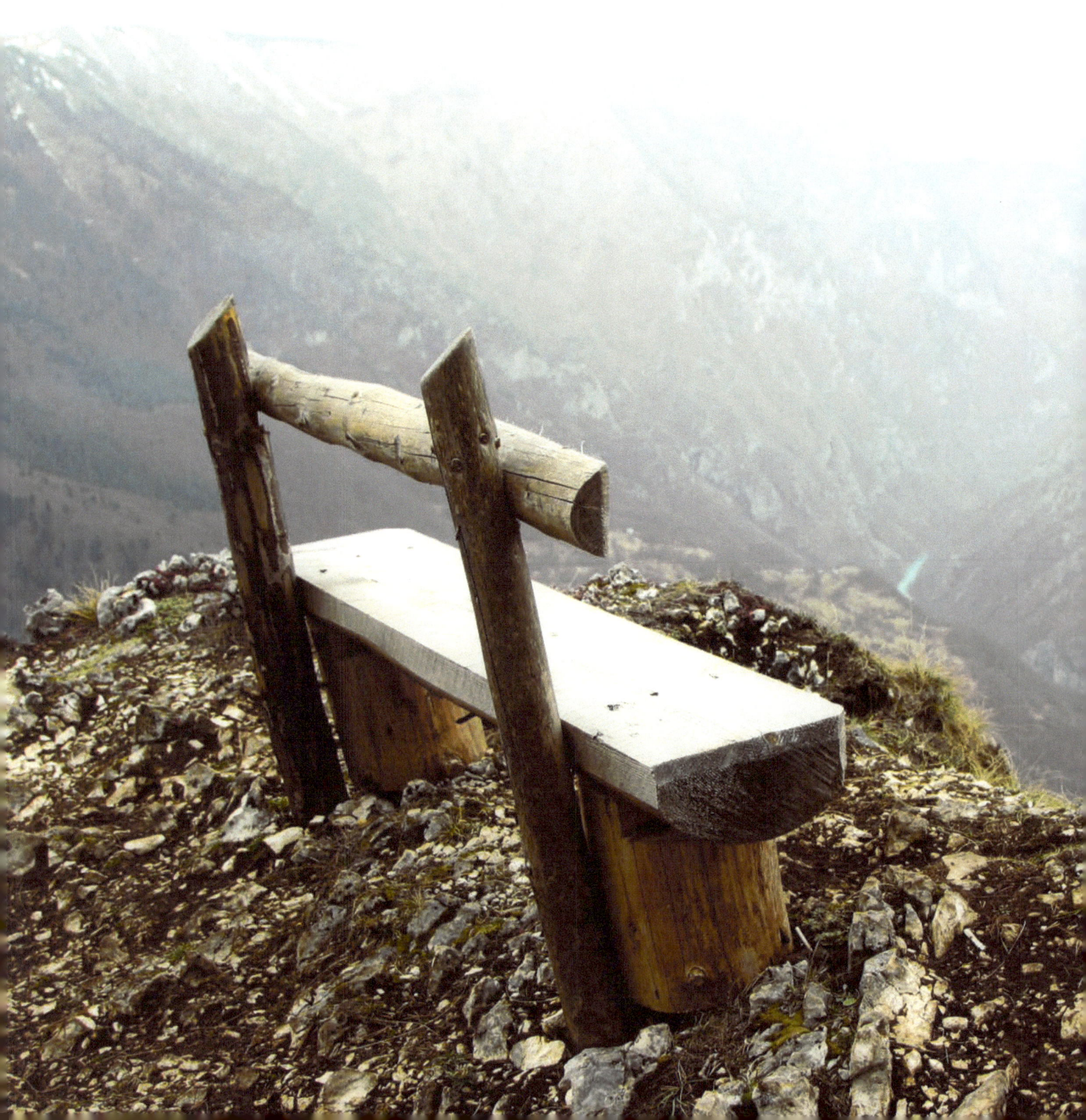

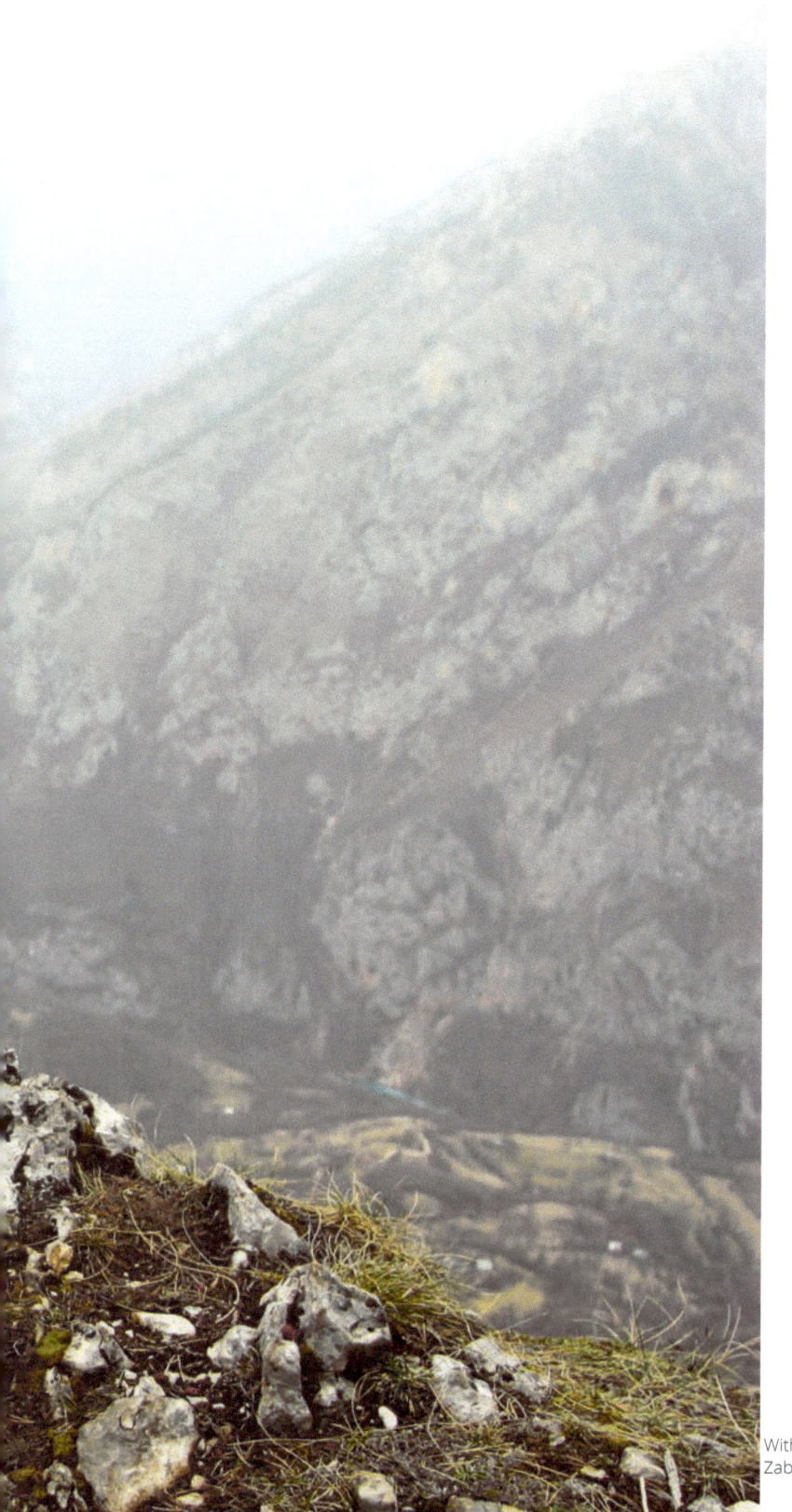

With you
Zabljak, February

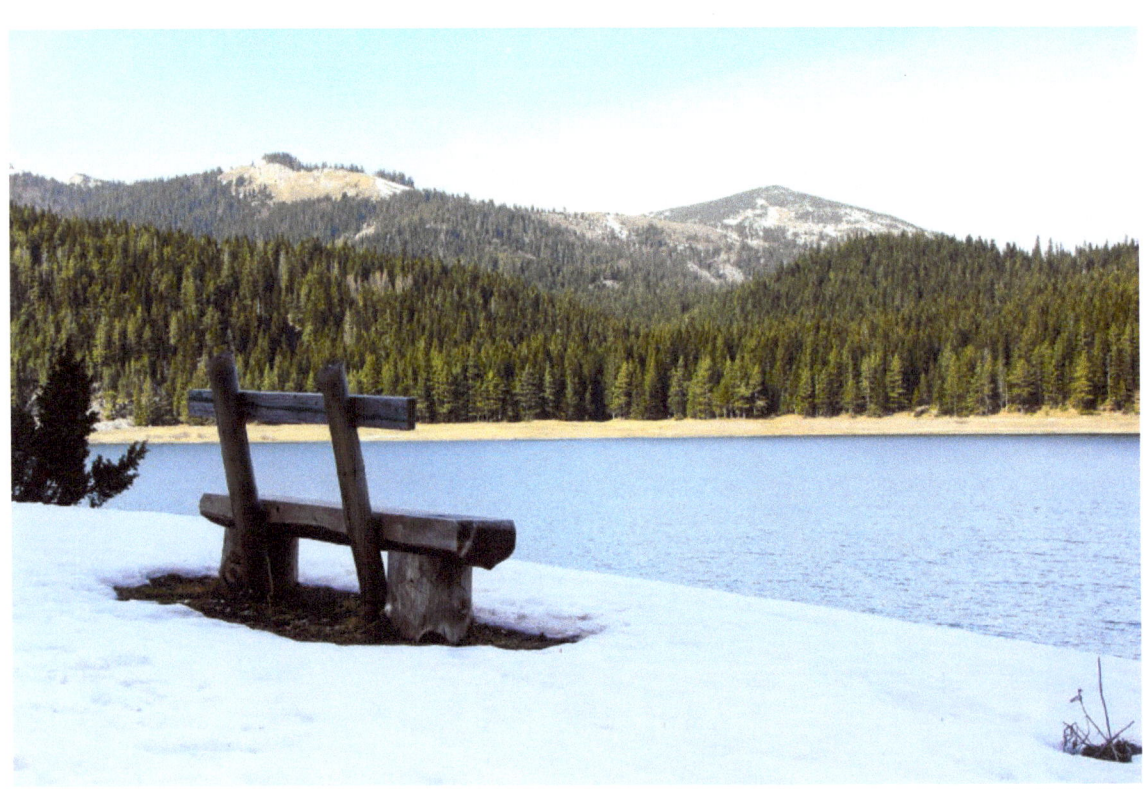

You're not there
Black lake, February

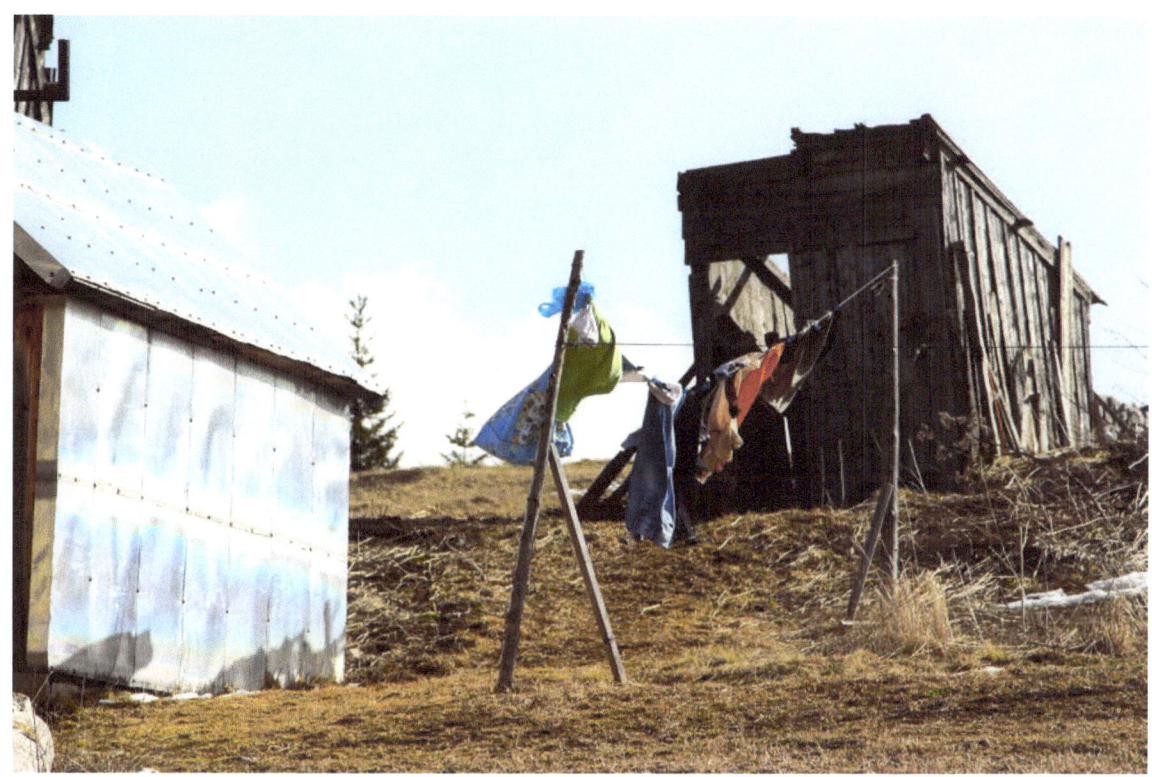

Hanging
Zabljak, February

SKADARSKO

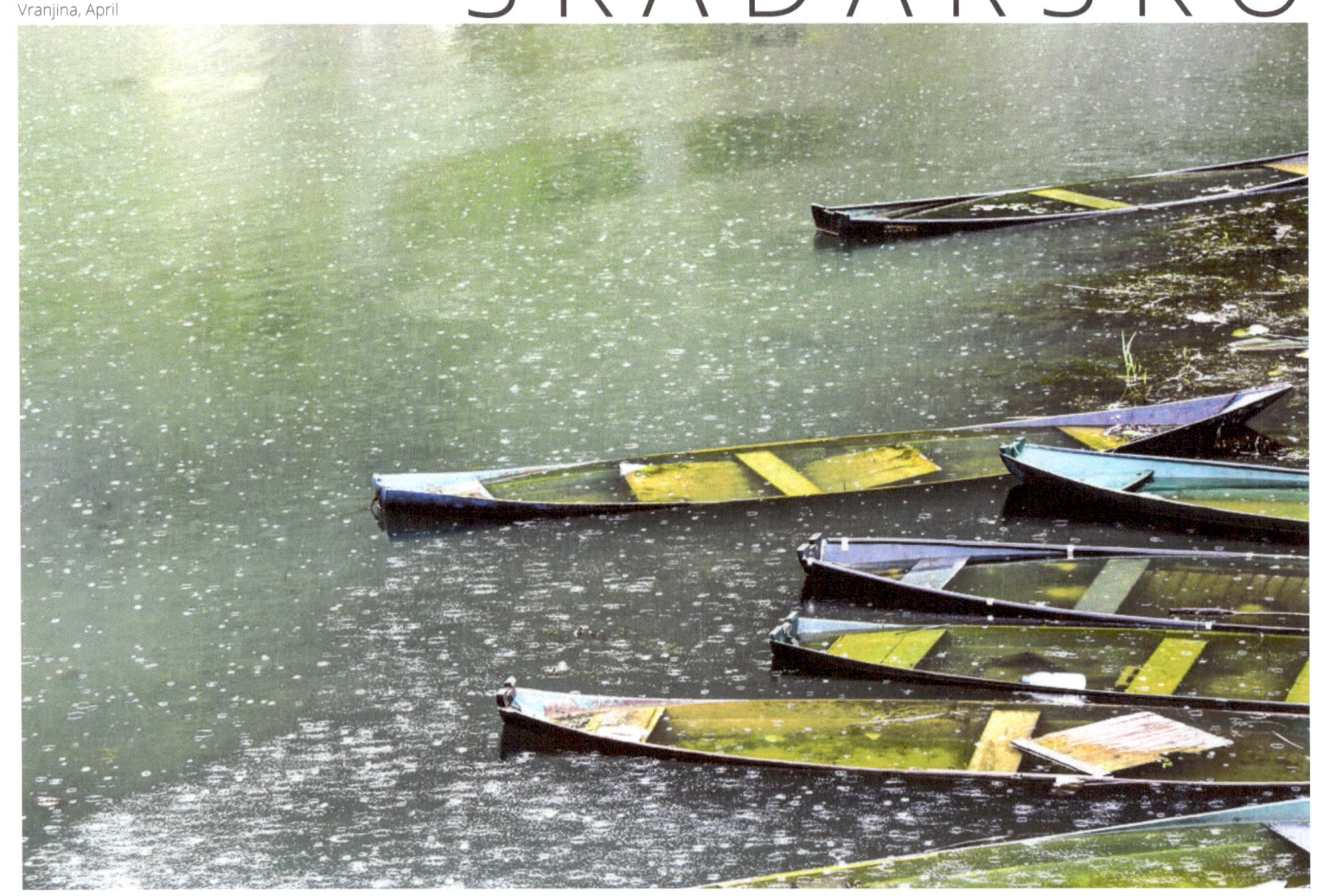

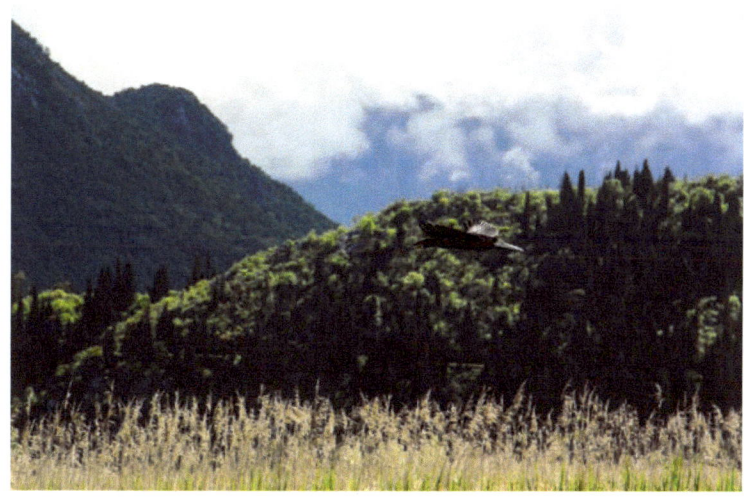

Fly away
Lake skadar, April

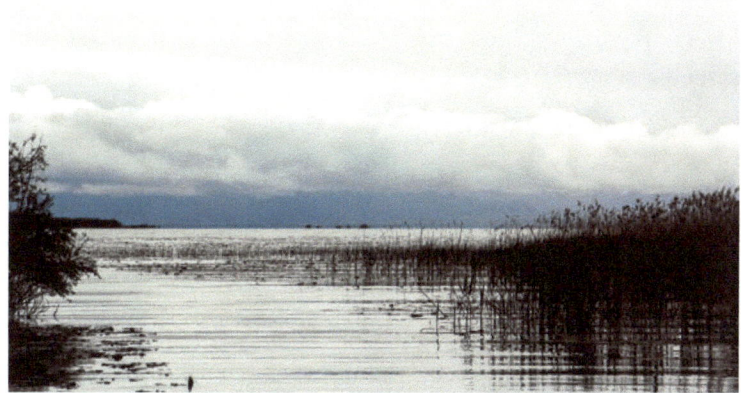

Here comes the sun
Lake skadar, April

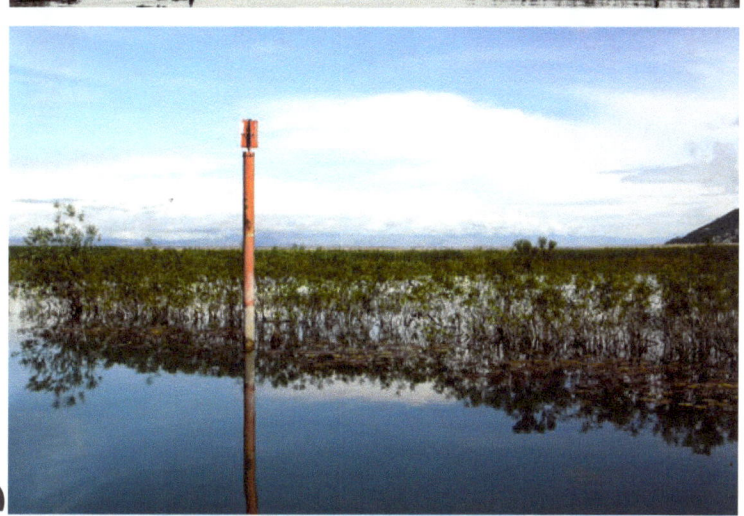

Reflection
Lake skadar, April

JEZERO

Mirror
Lake skadar, April
(next page)

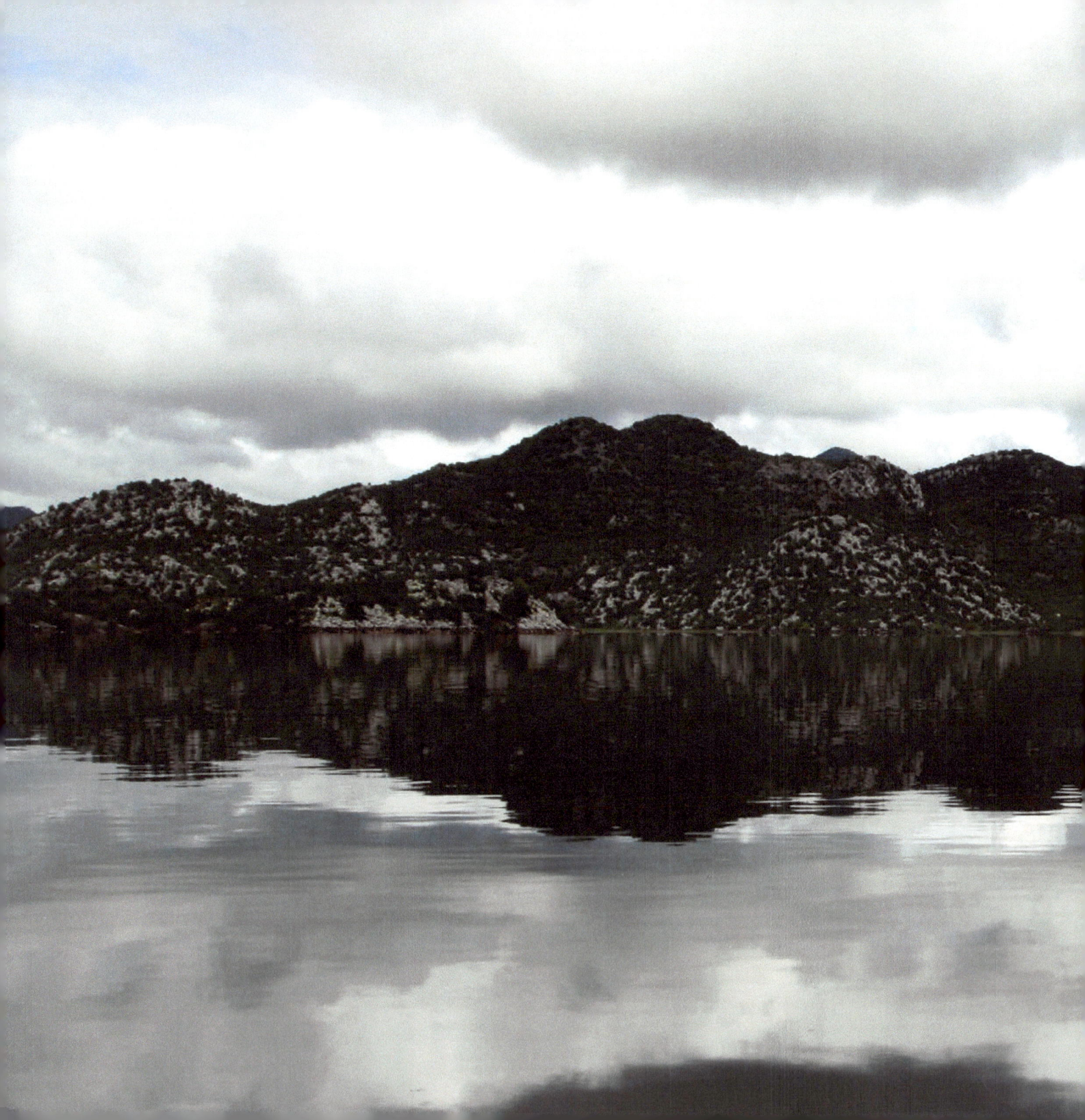

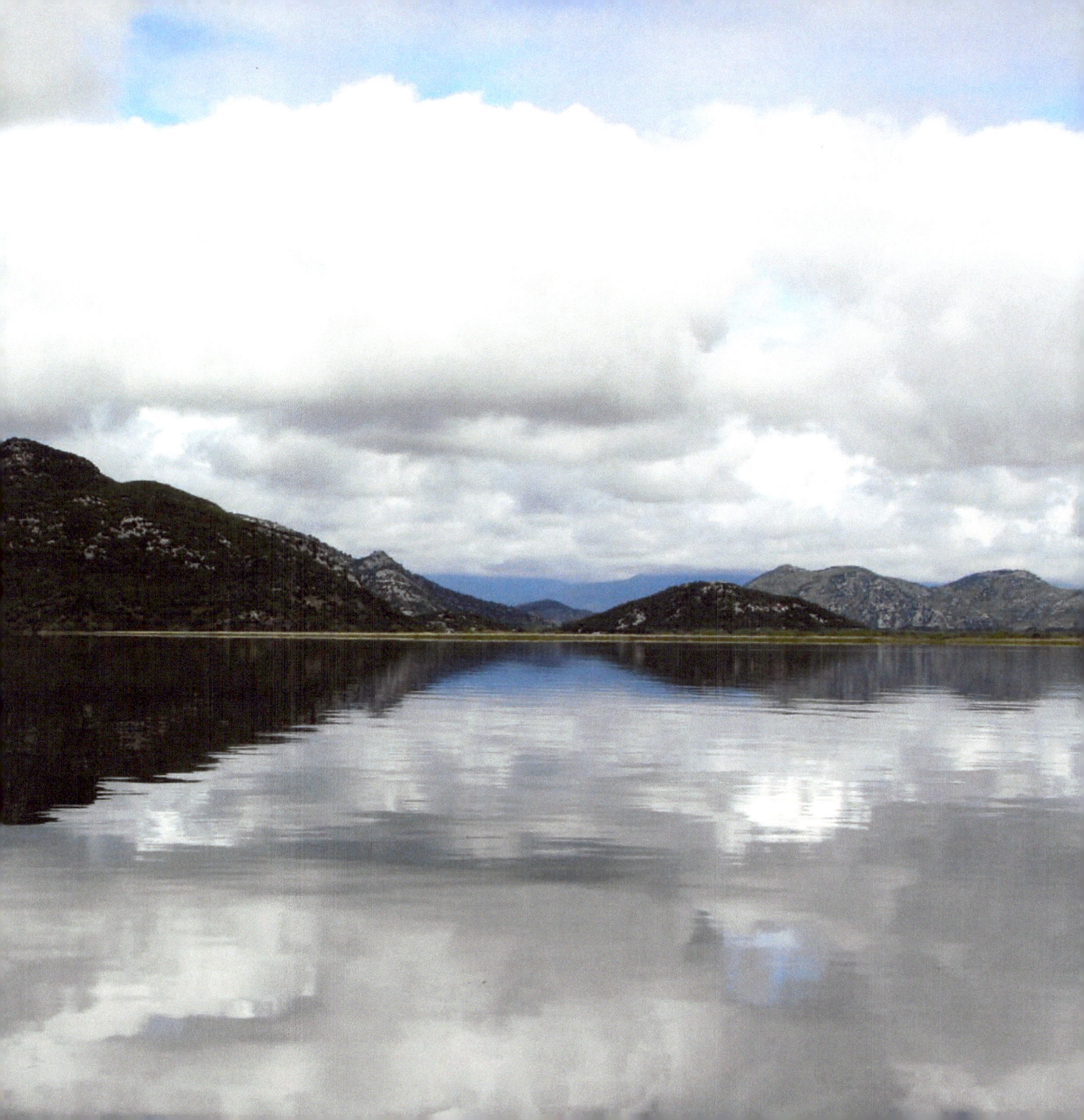

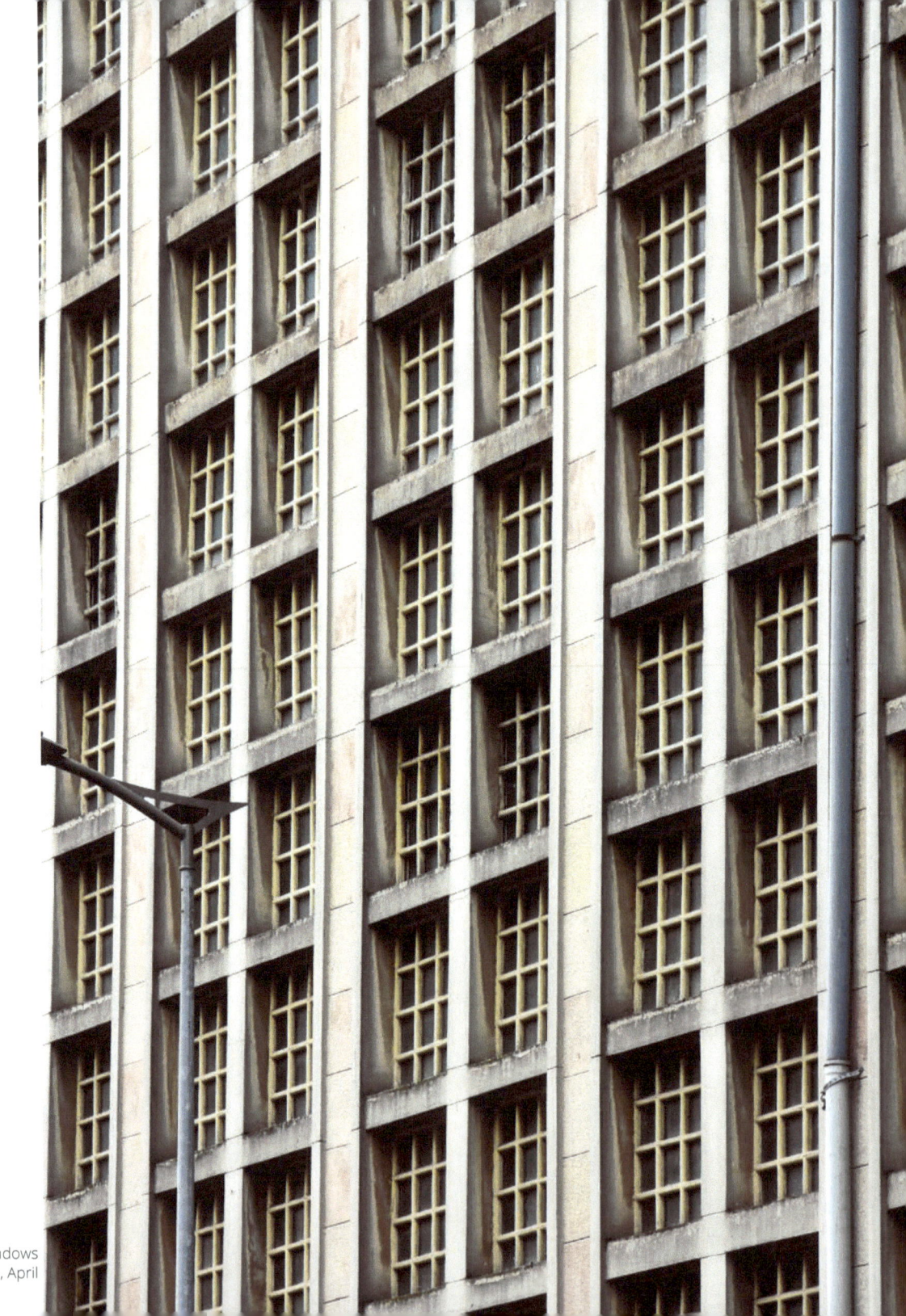

Windows
Podgorica, April

PODGORICA

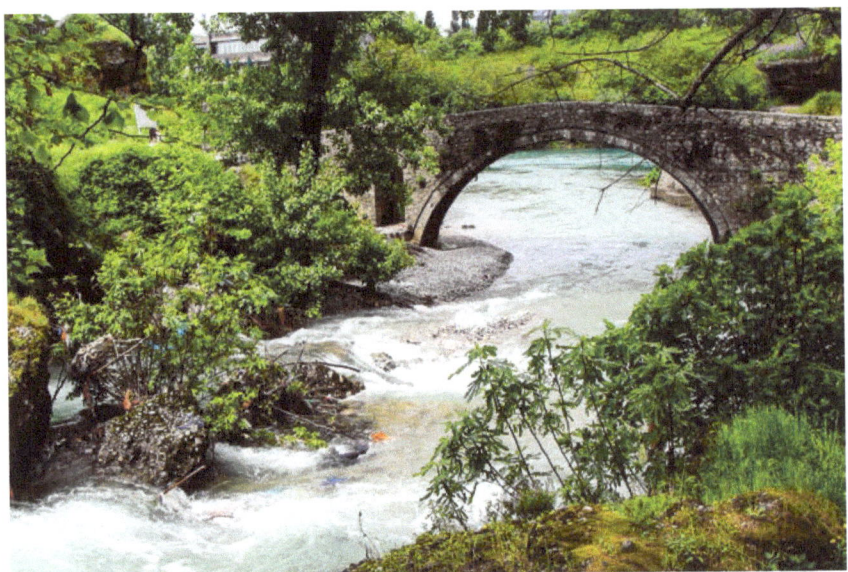

The bridge
Podgorica, May

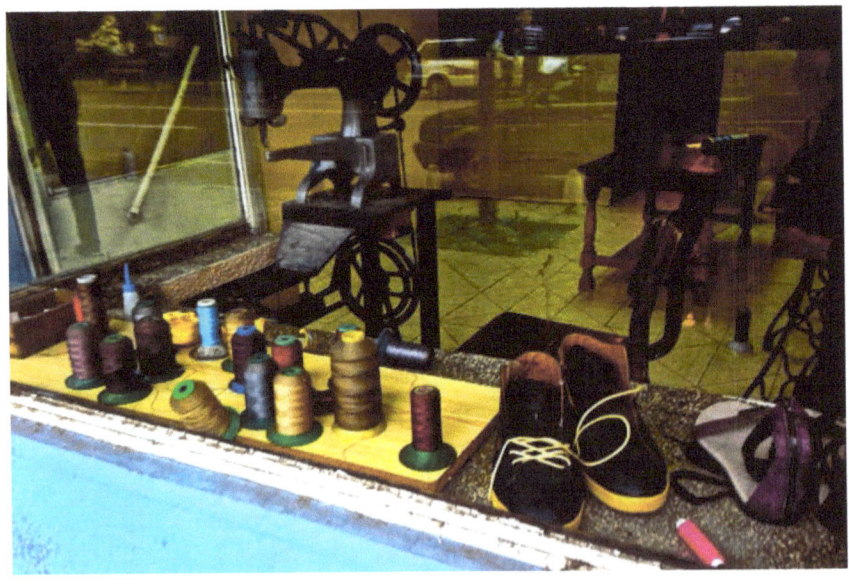

Needlework
Podgorica, May

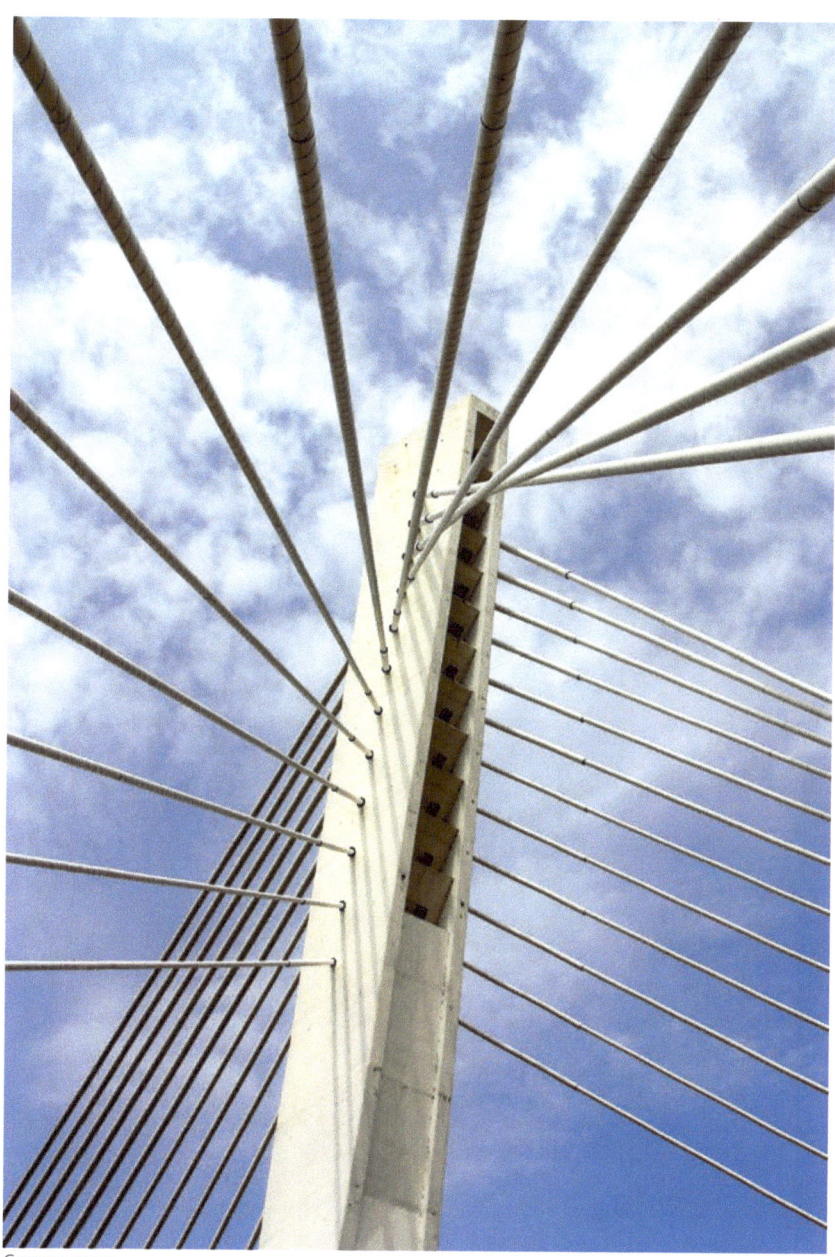

Convergence
Podgorica, April

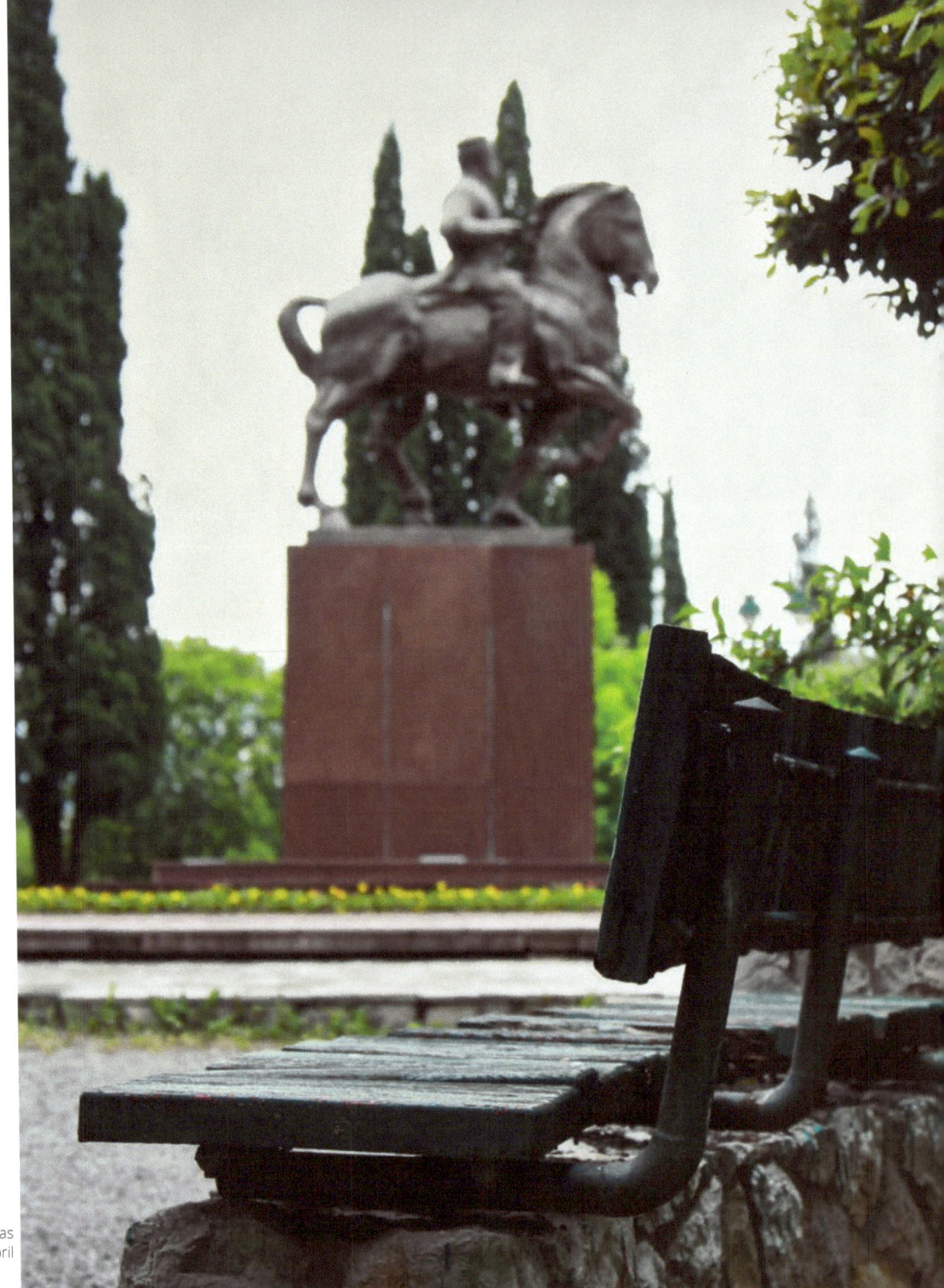

Nicholas
Podgorica, April

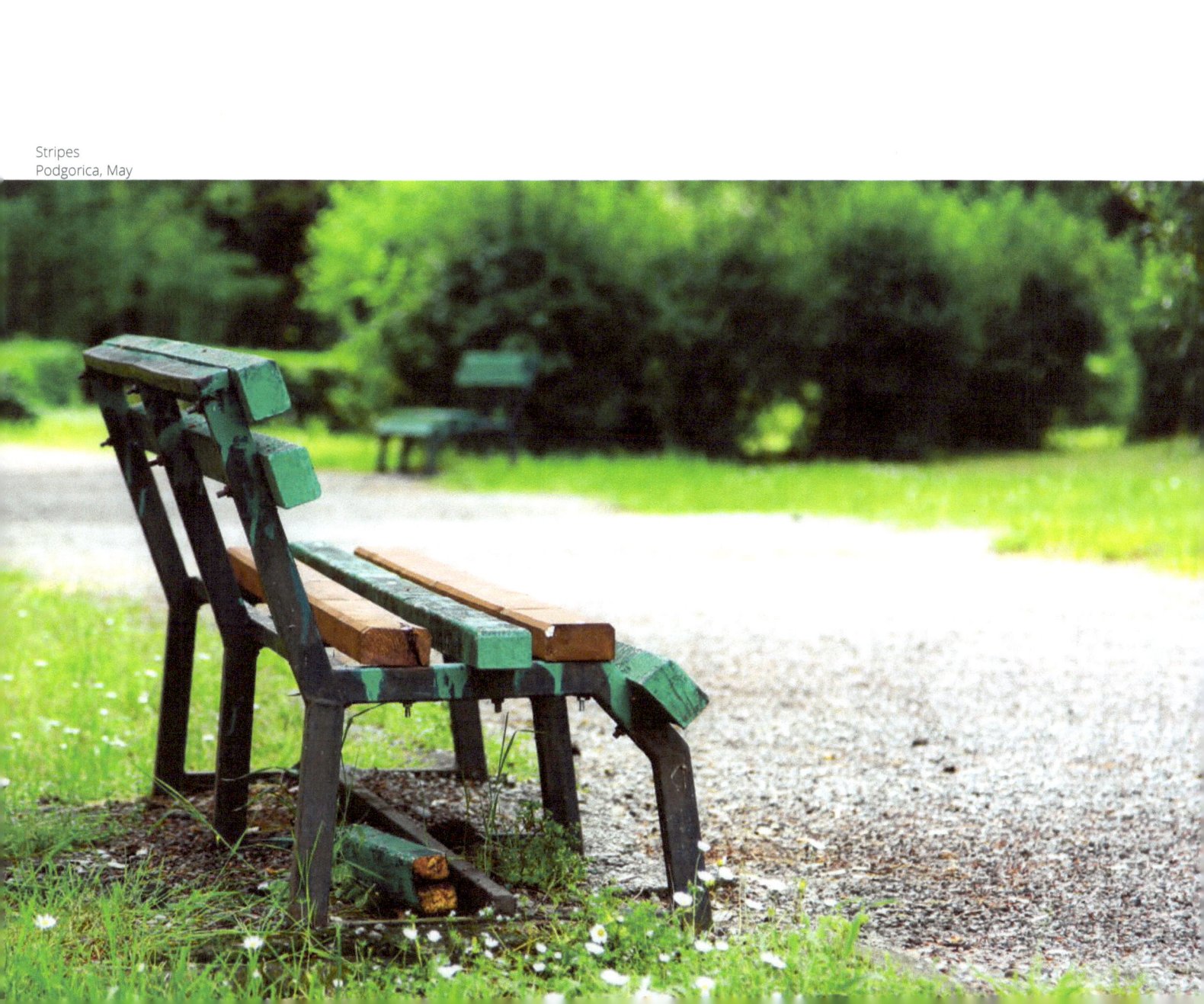

Stripes
Podgorica, May

Rainbow
Cetinje, May

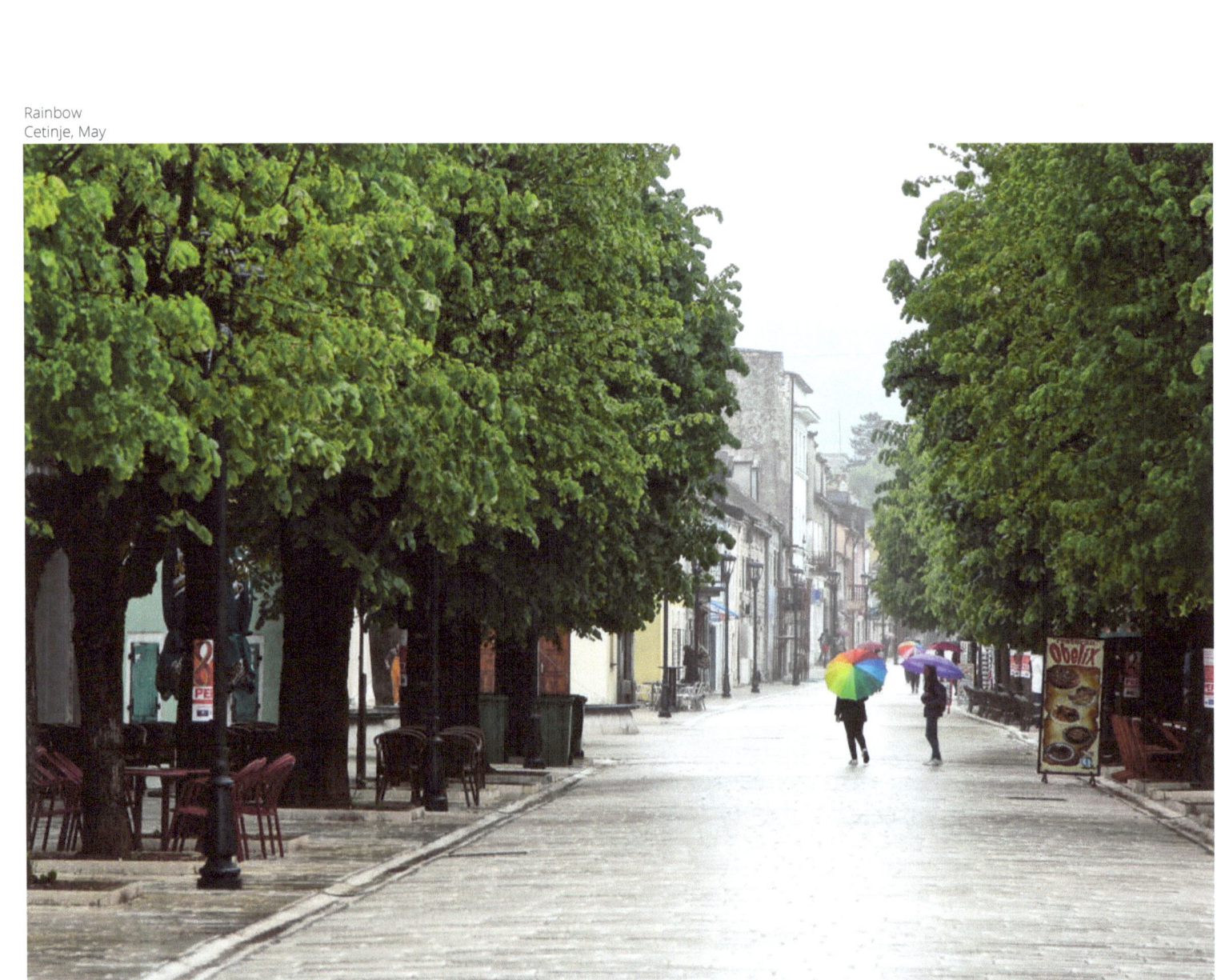

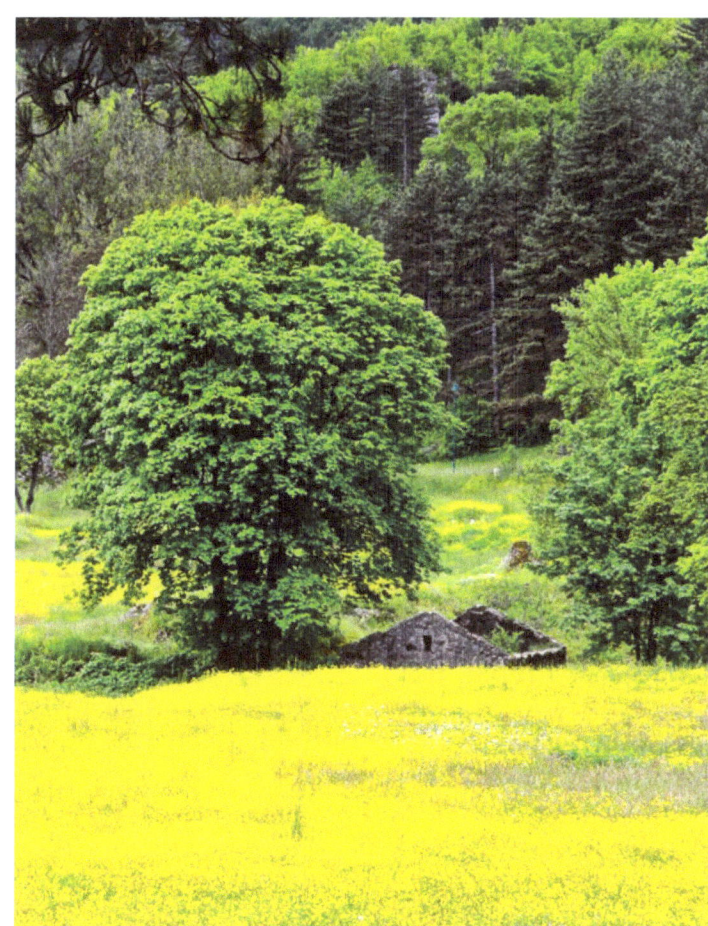

Yellow
Cetinje, May

C E T I N J E

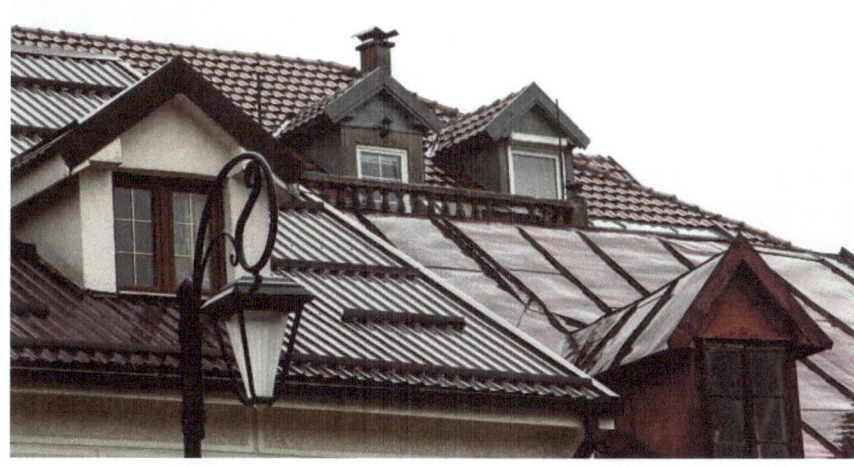

Watching
Cetinje, May

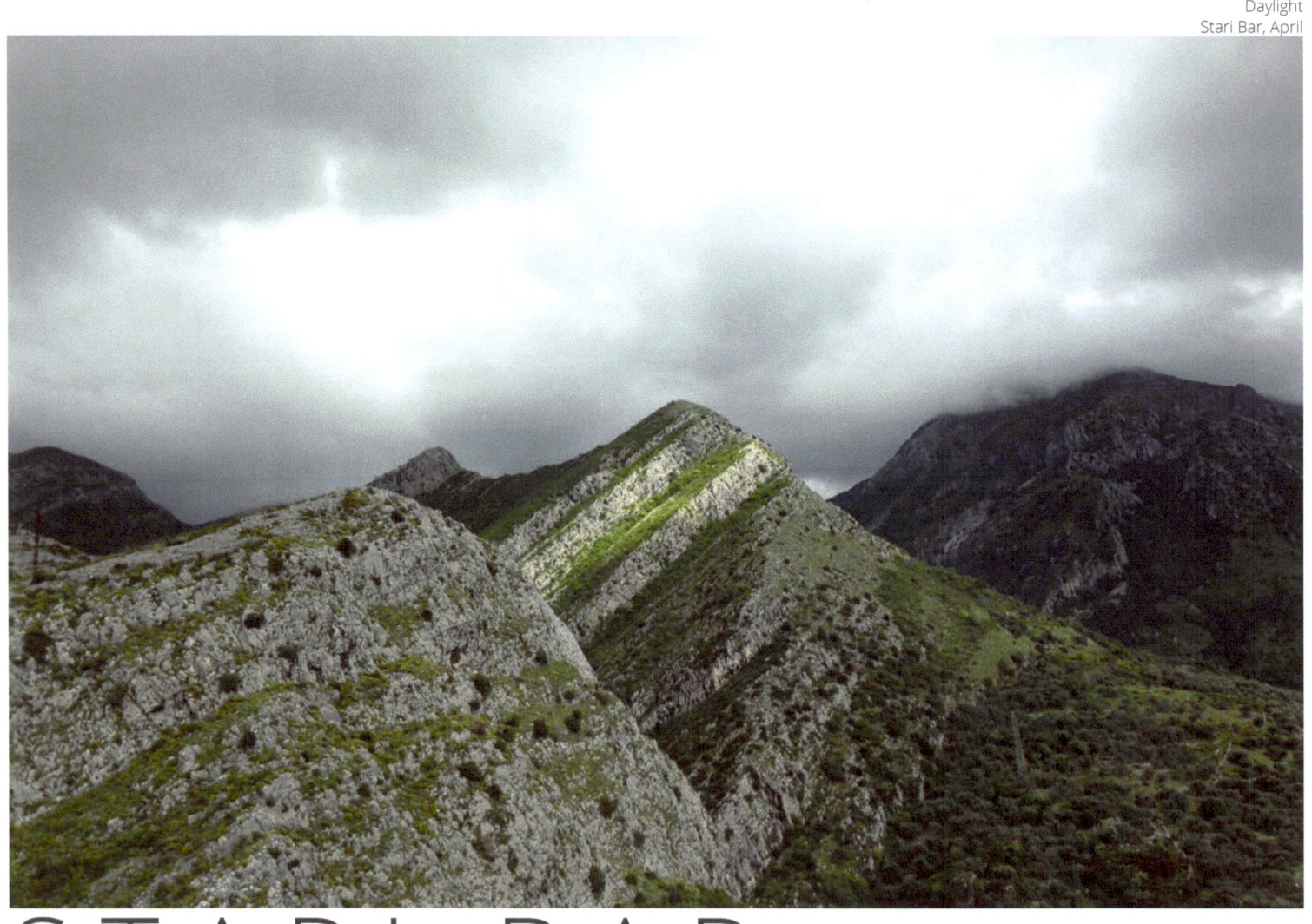

S T A R I   B A R

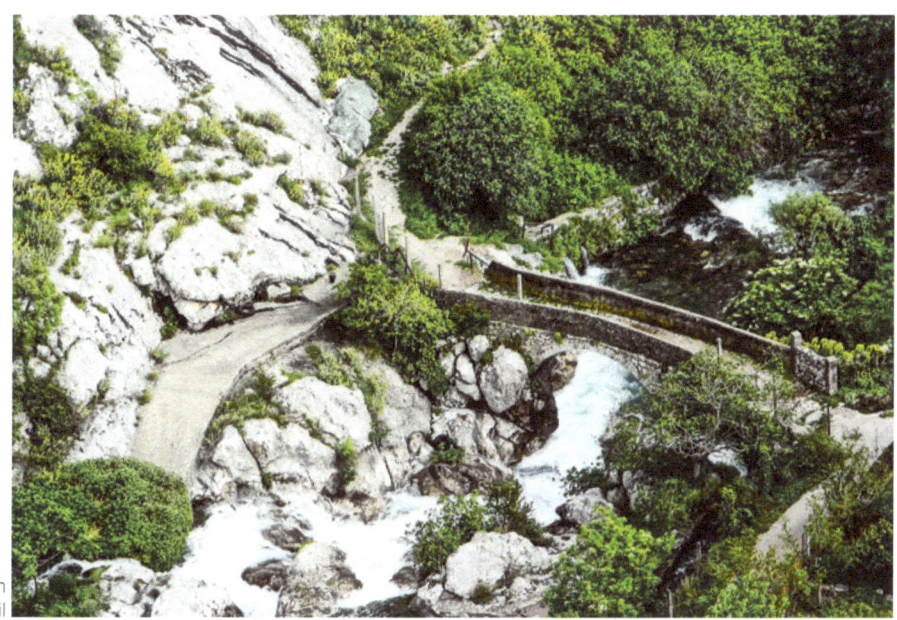

Stream
Stari Bar, April

Clock
Stari Bar, April

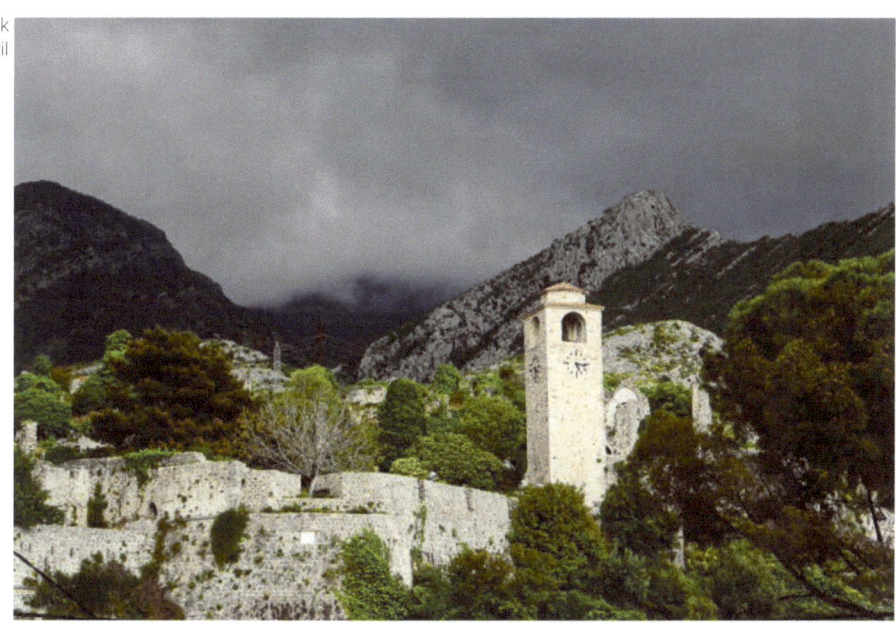

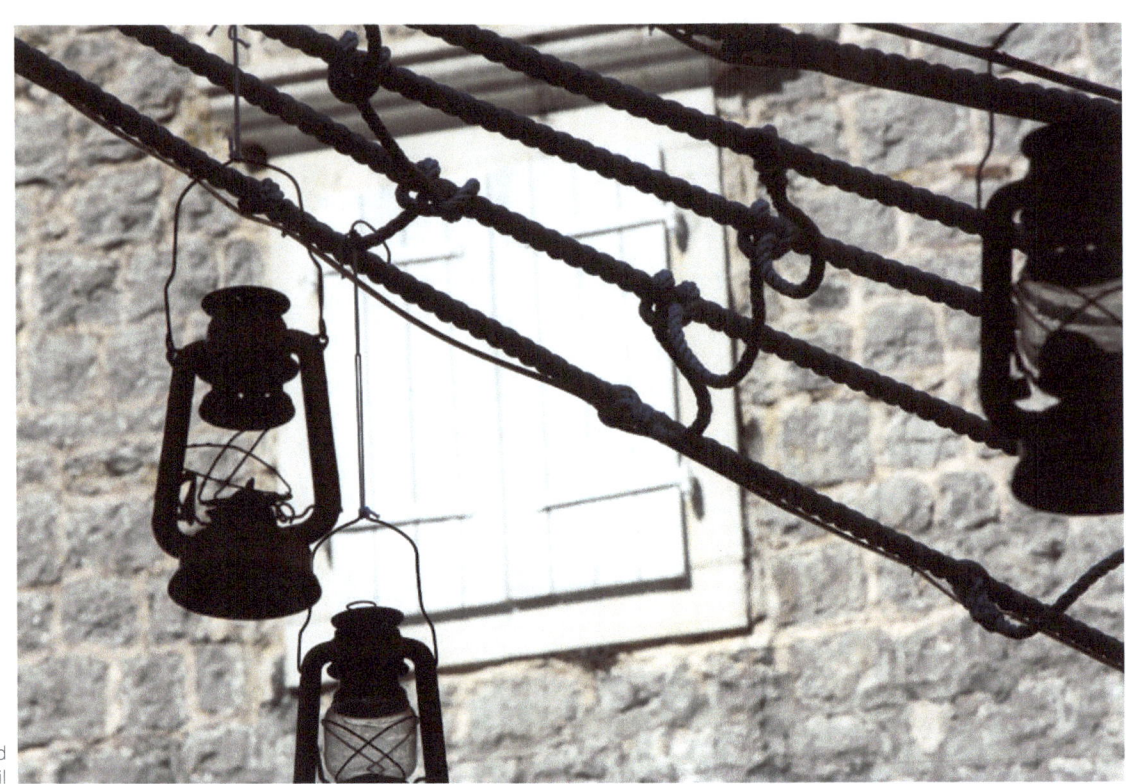

Closed
Budva, April

Taboo
Sveti Stefan, April

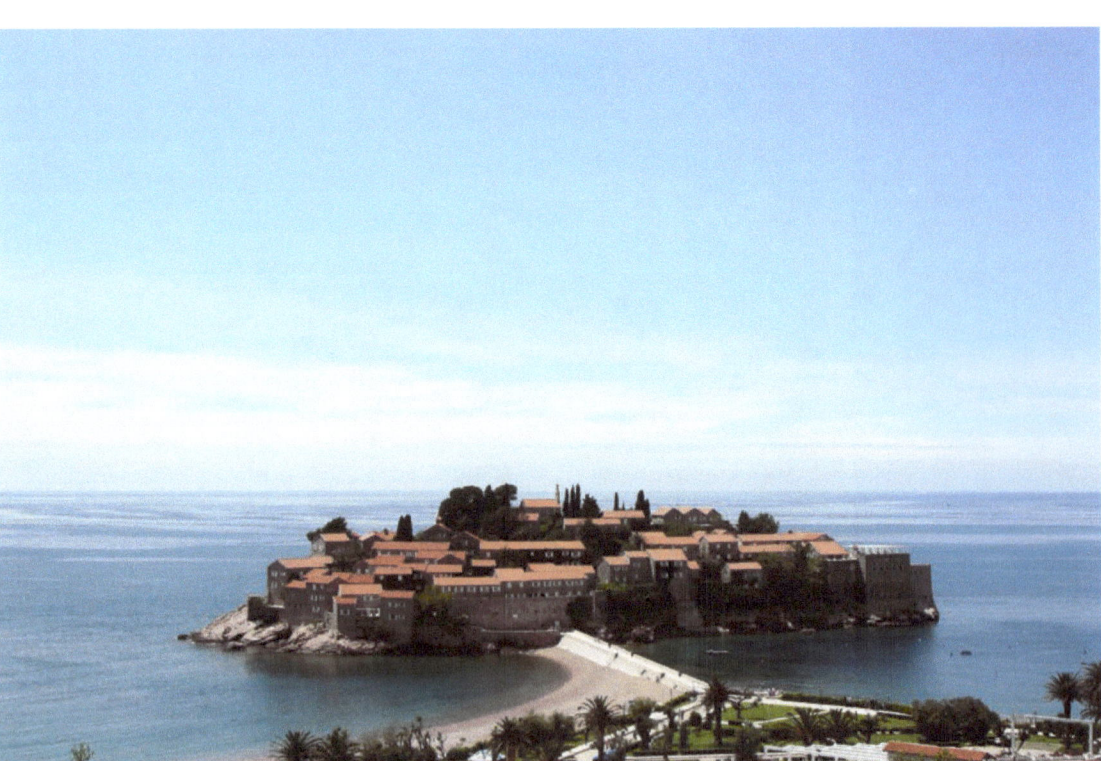

BUDVA

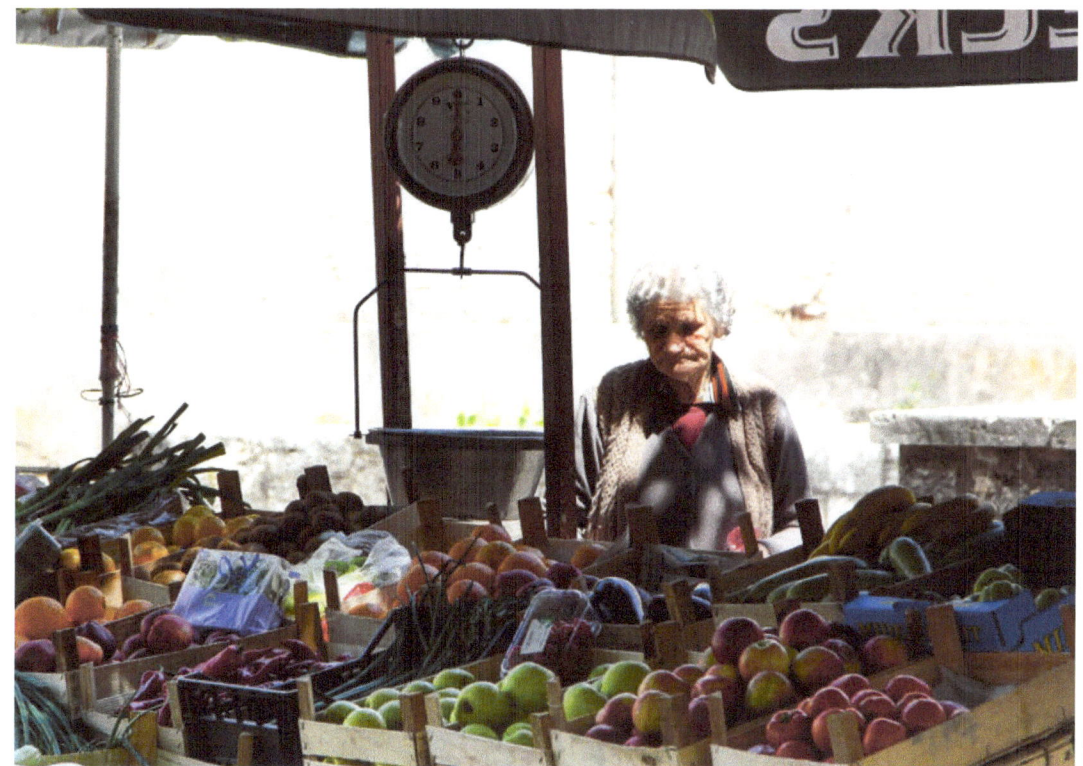

Balance
Risan, May

Lighthouse
Kamenari, May

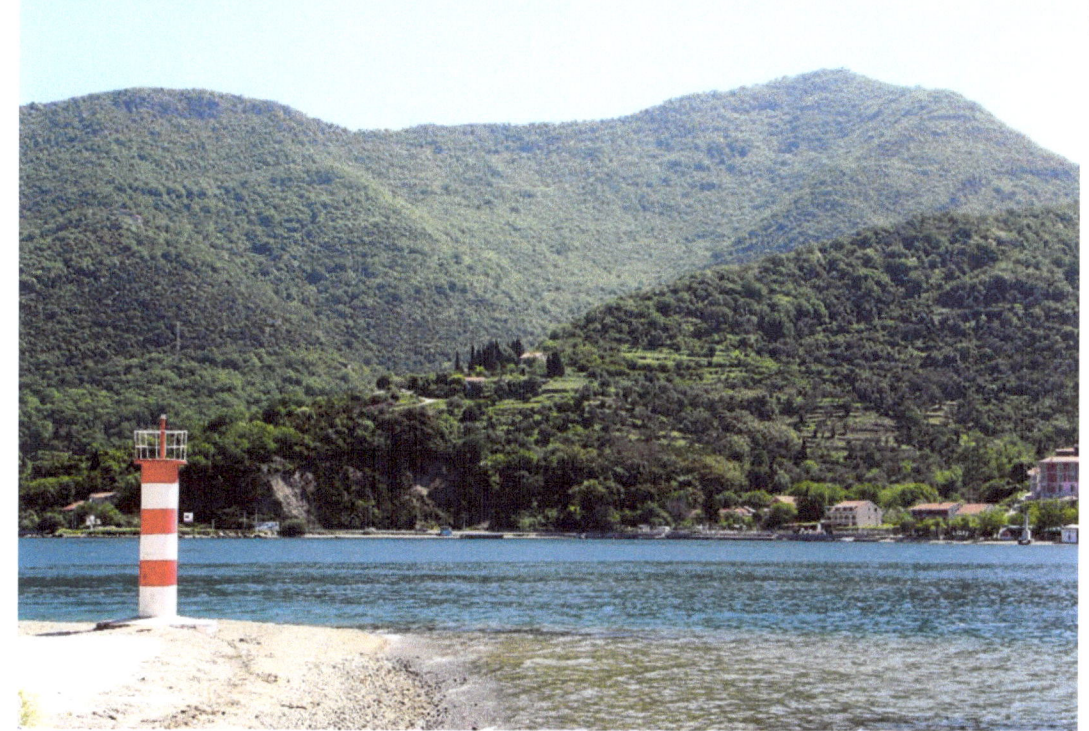

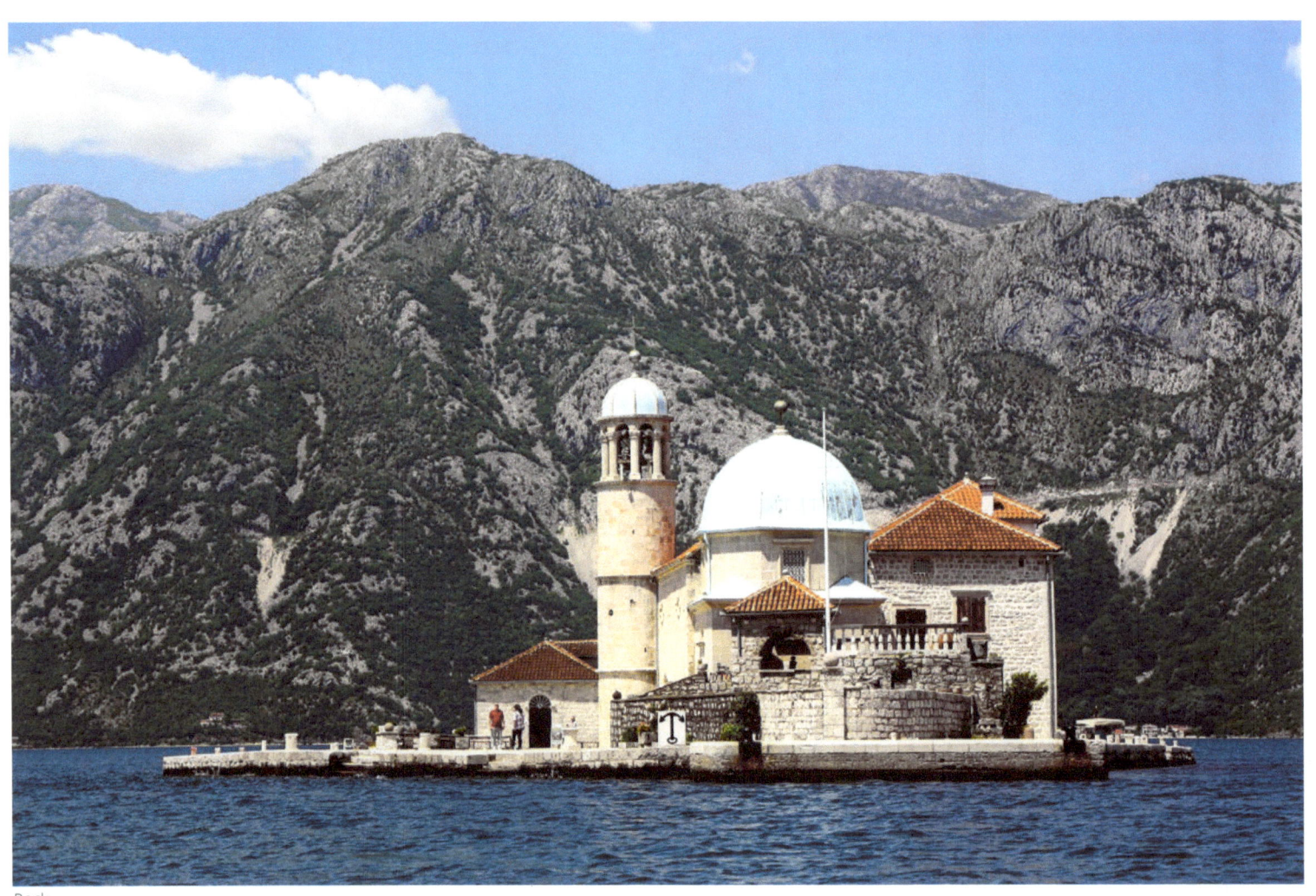

Rock
Our Lady of the Rocks, May

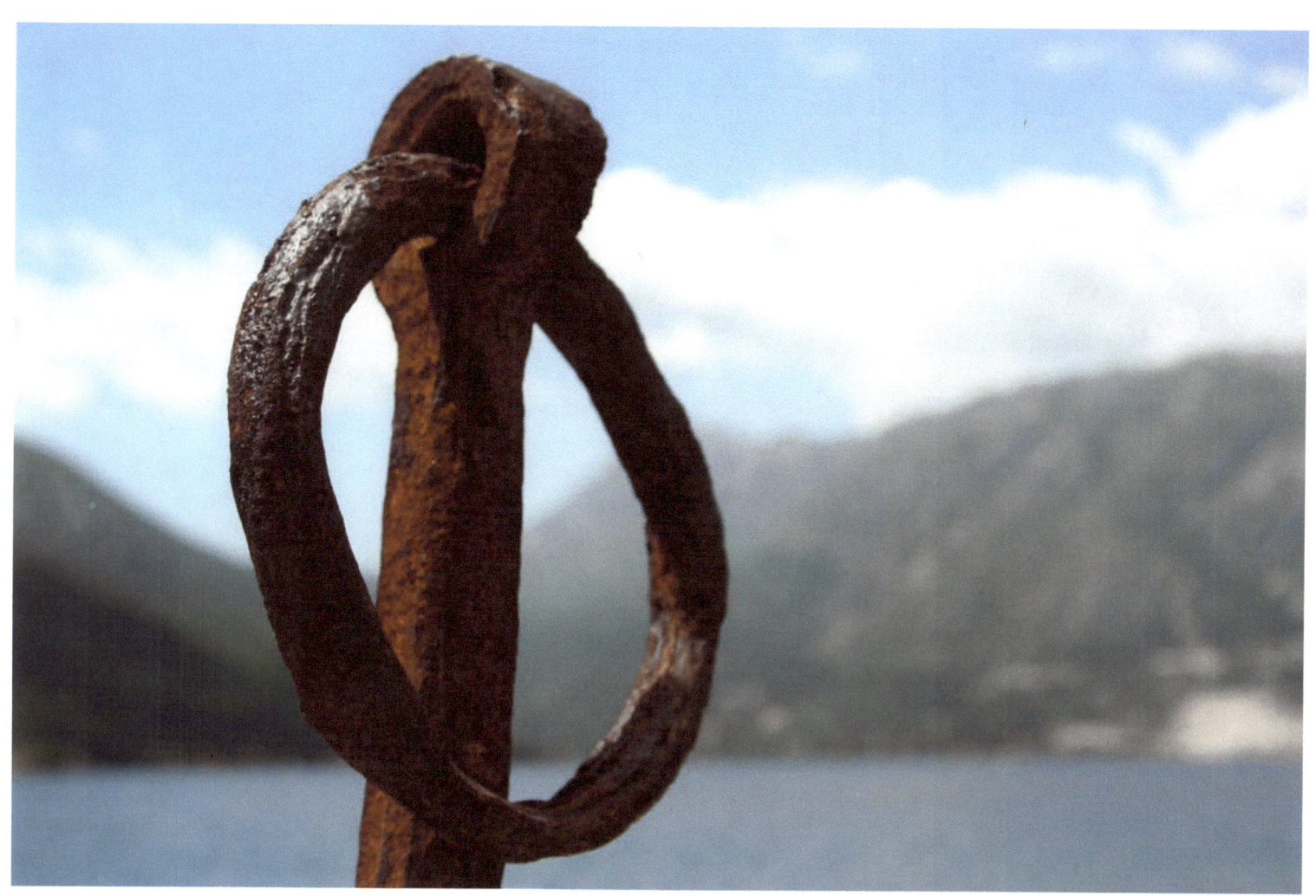

Rust
Our Lady of the Rocks, May

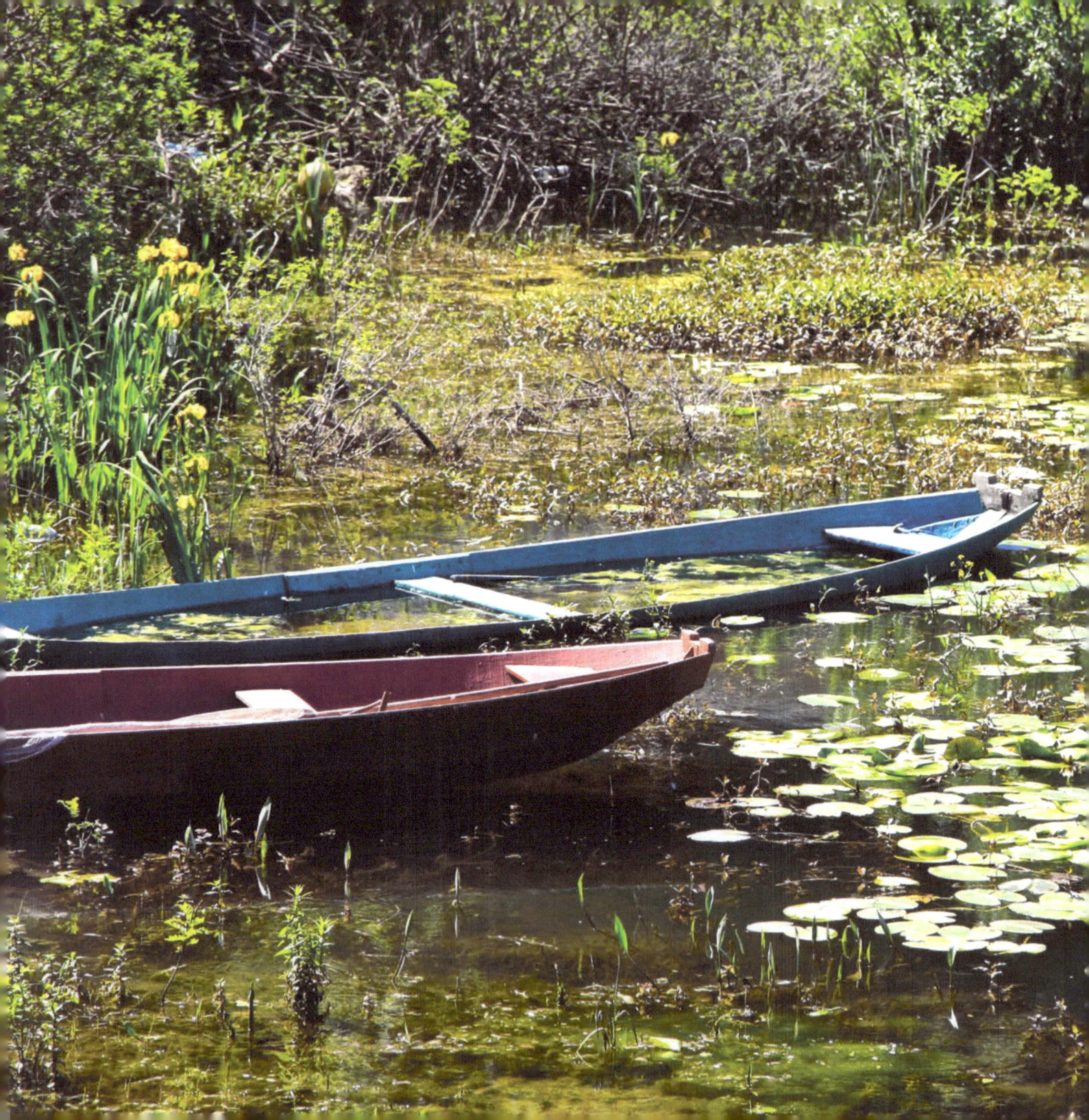

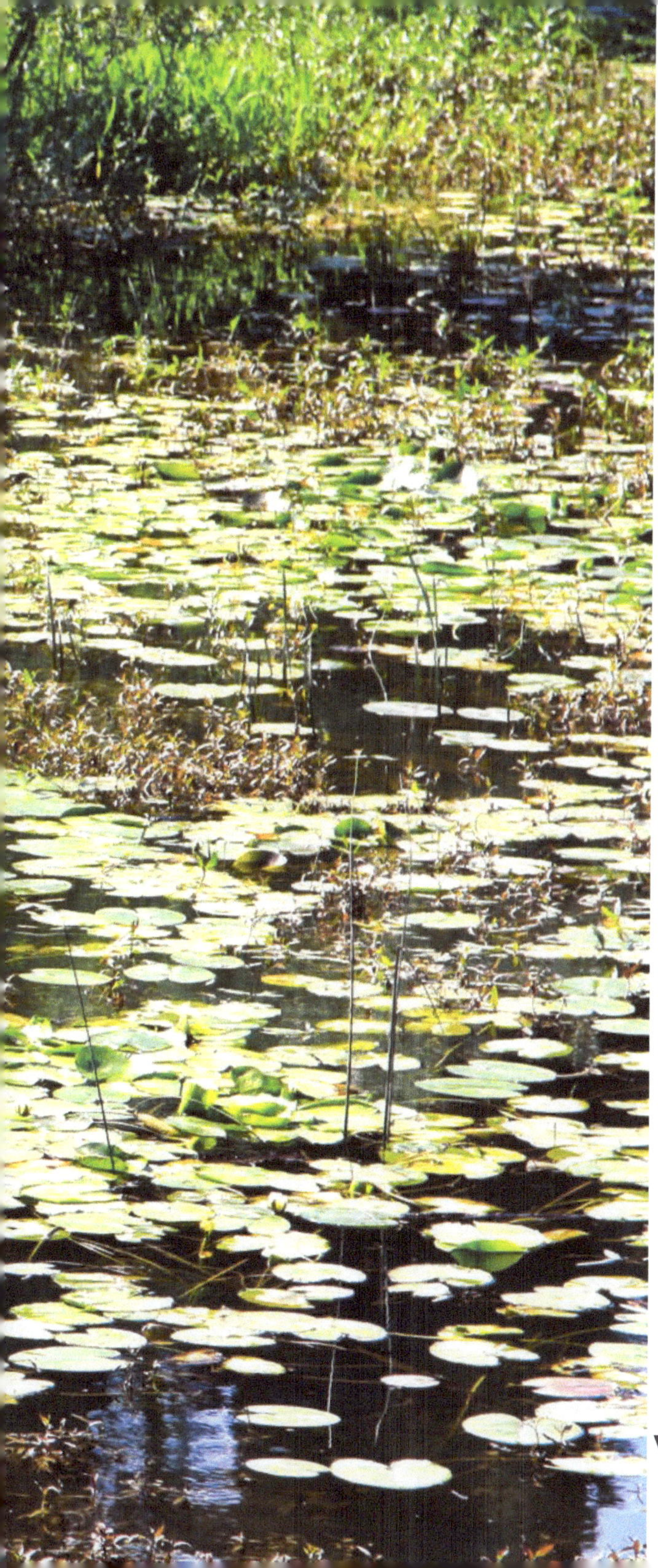

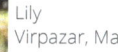

Lily
Virpazar, May

VIRPAZAR

ULCINJ

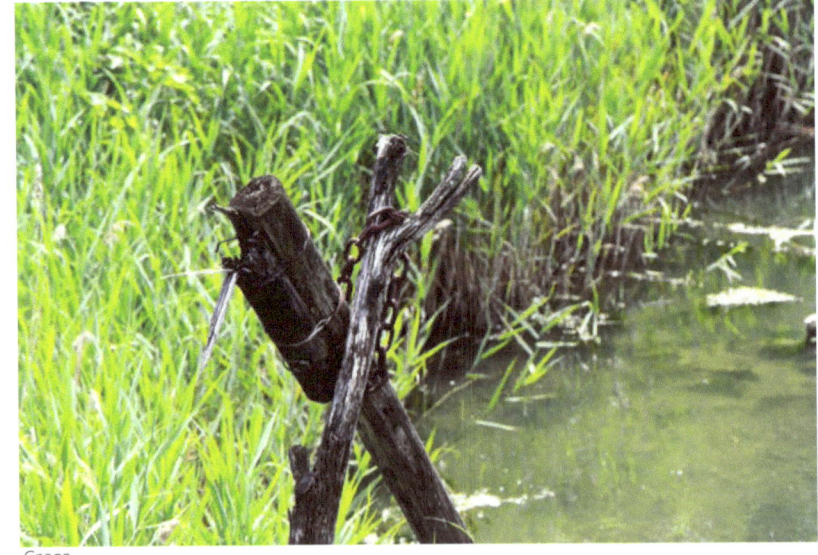

Cross
Ulcinj, May

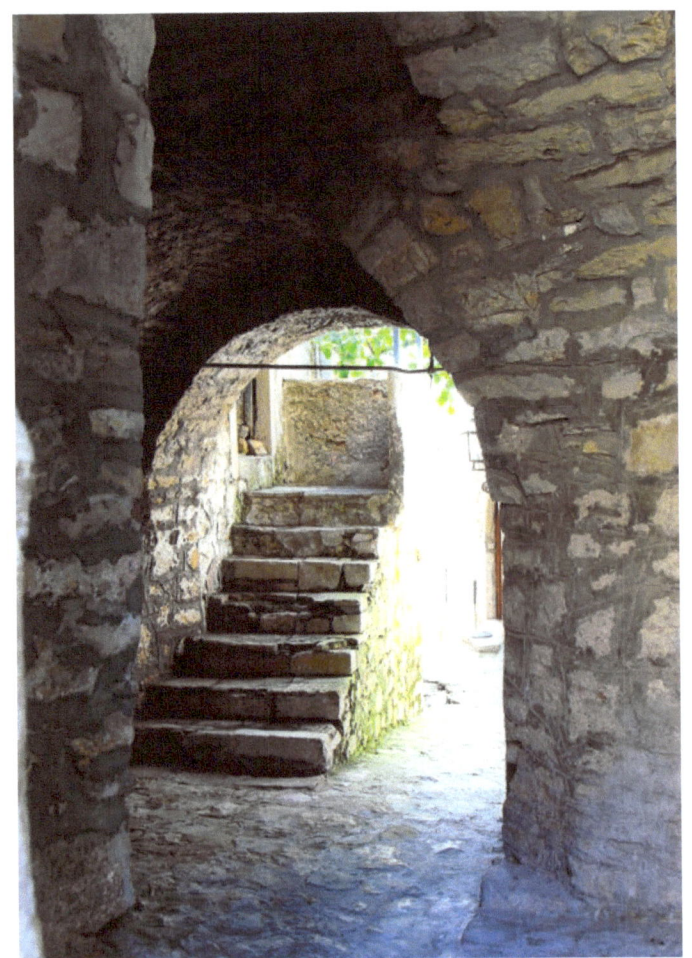

Shadow
Ulcinj, May

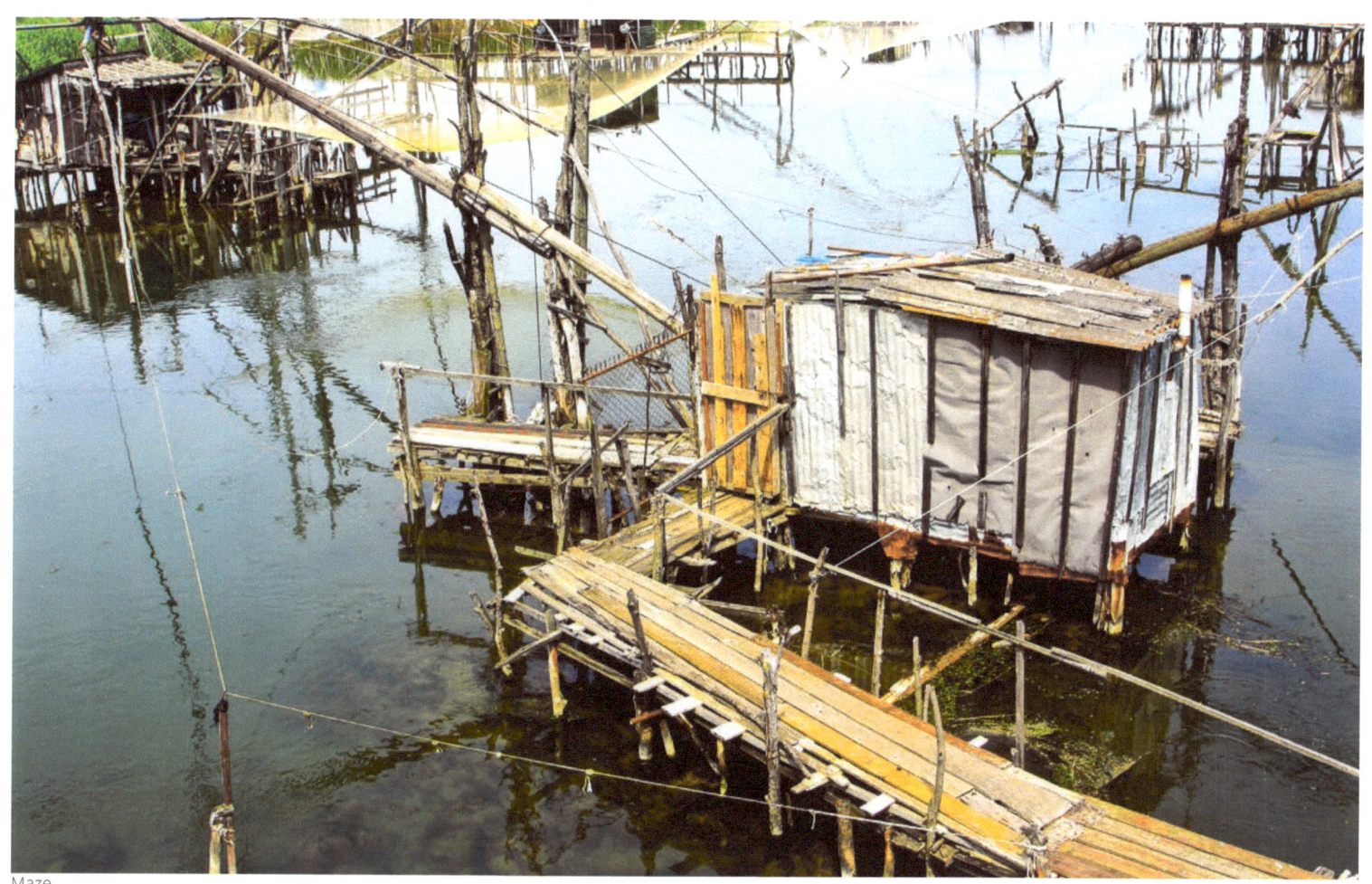

Maze
Ulcinj, May

RIJEKA

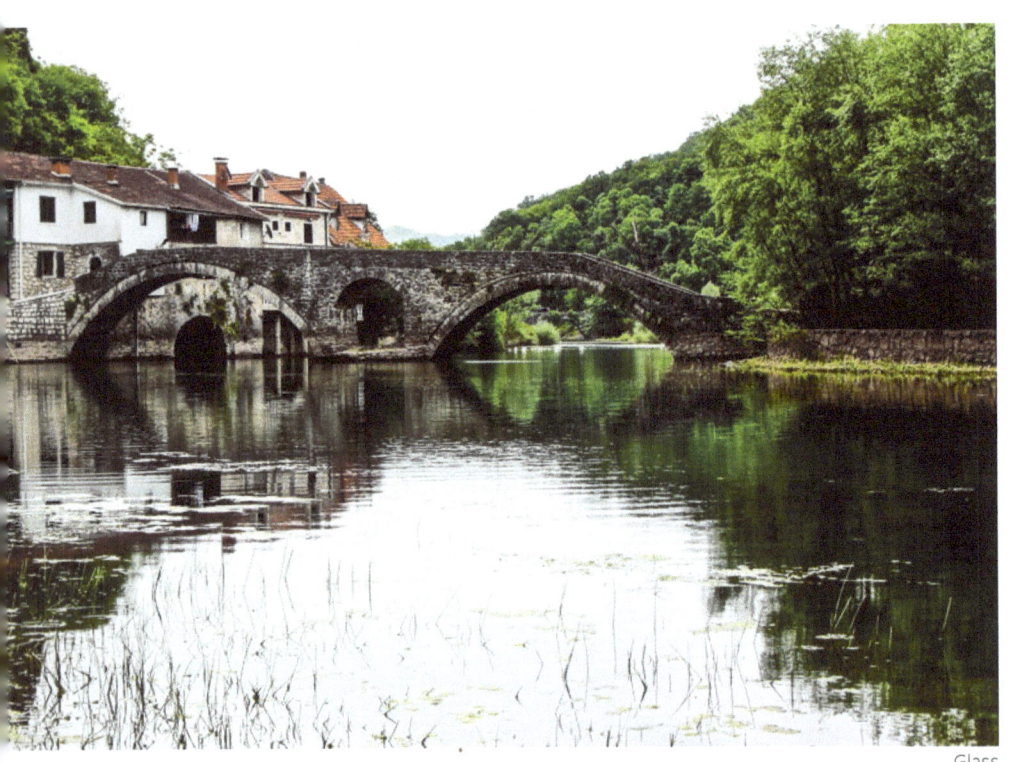

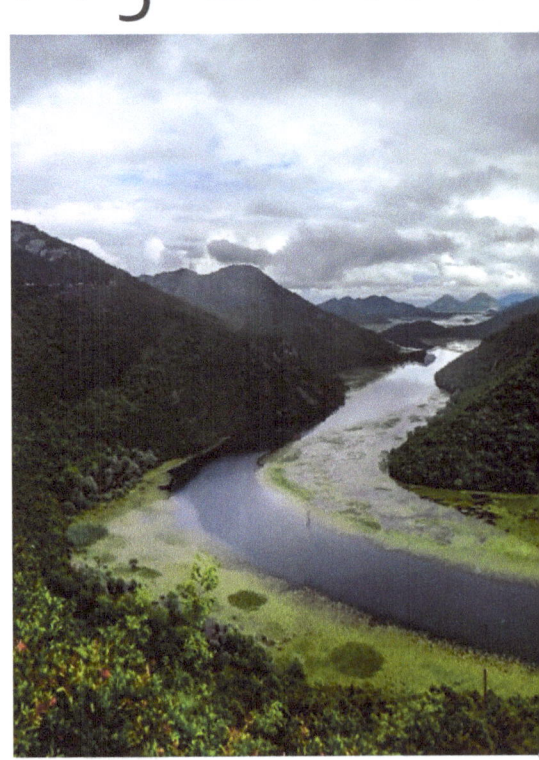

Glass
Rijeka Crojevica, May

Bend
Rijeka Crojevica, May, May

CRNOJEVIĆA

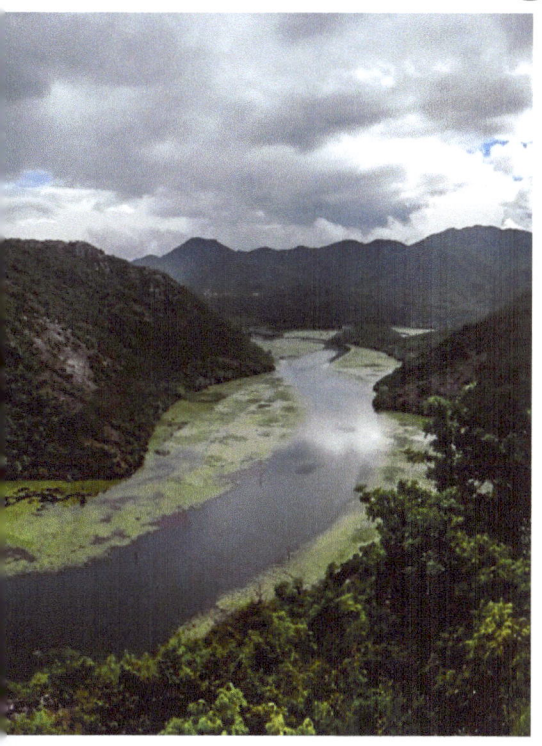

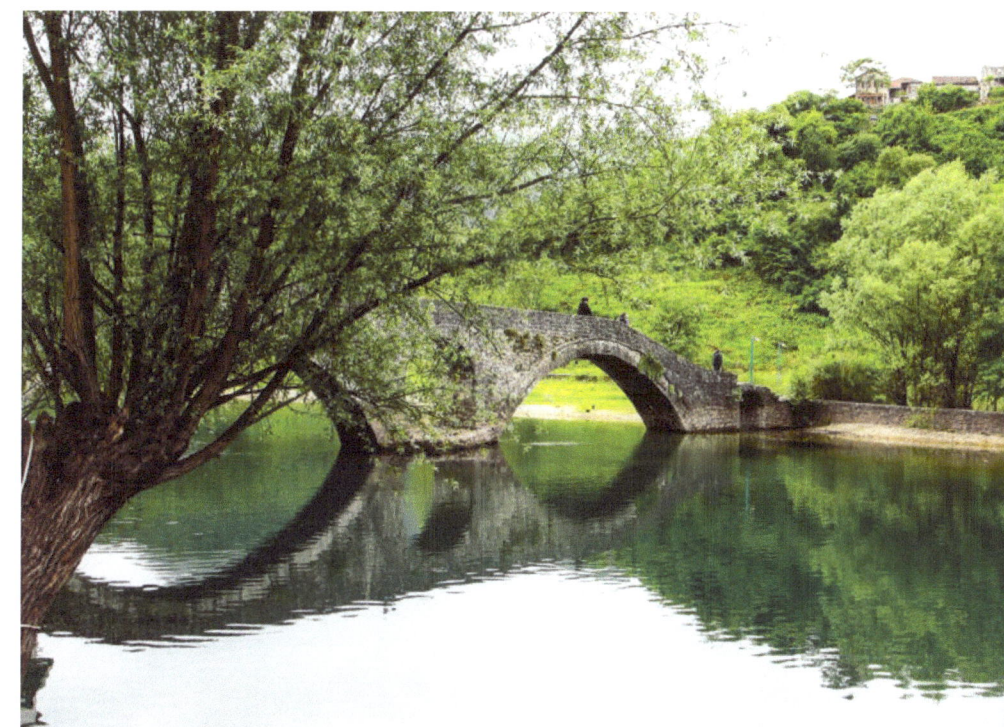

Greenpeace
Rijeka Crojevica, May

Twins
Rijeka Crojevica, May
(next page)

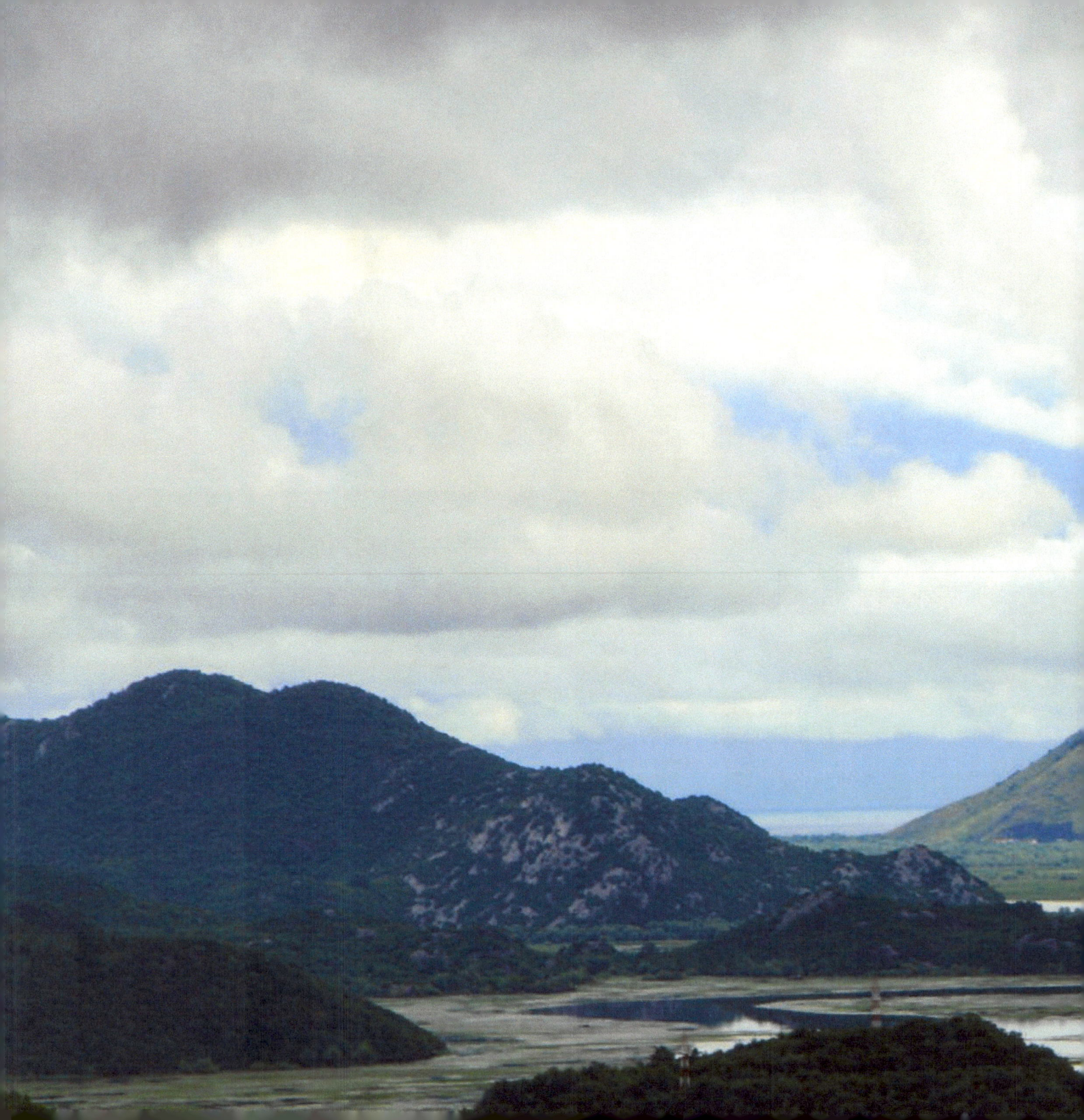

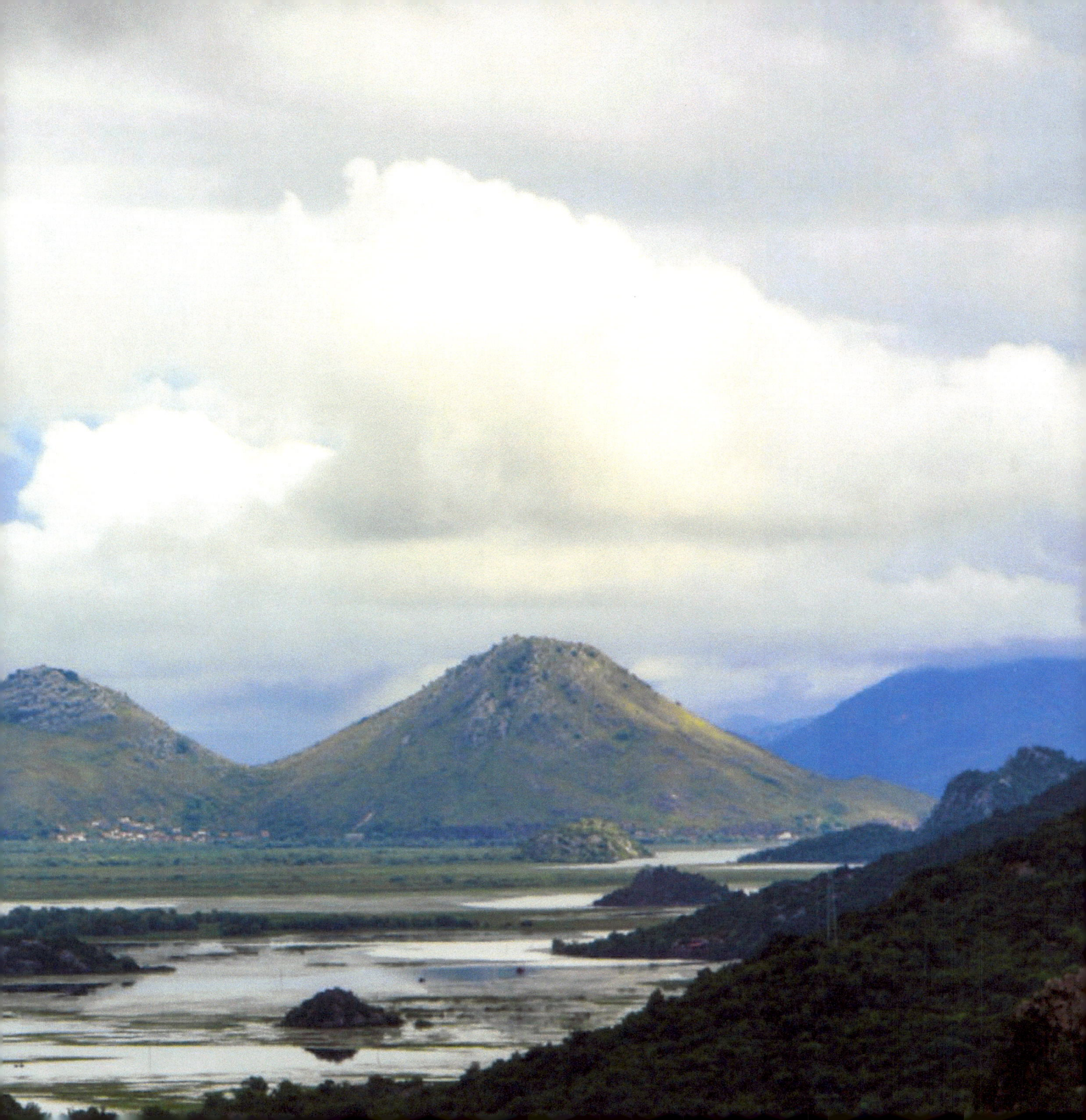

Deep blue
Rijeka Crojevica, May

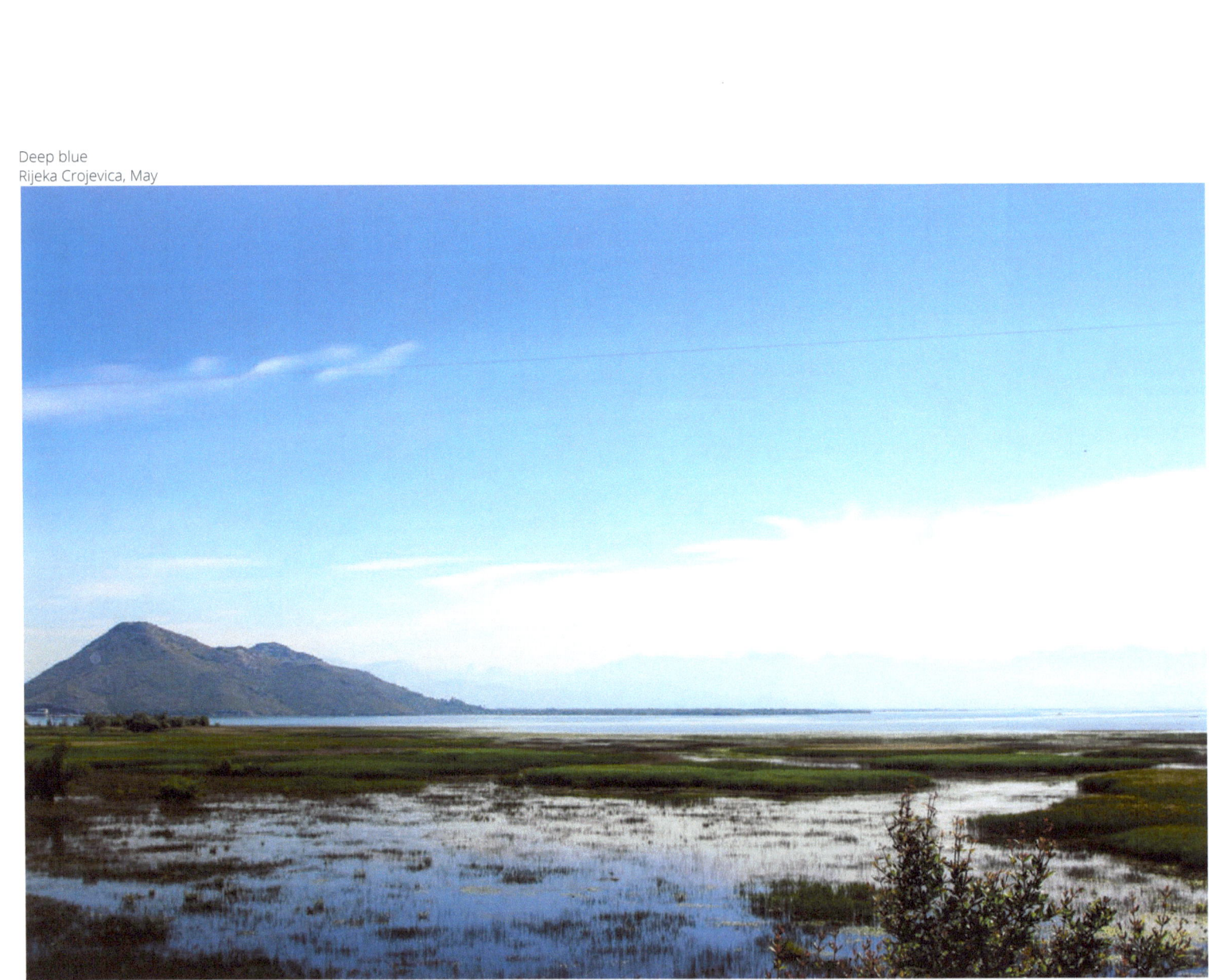

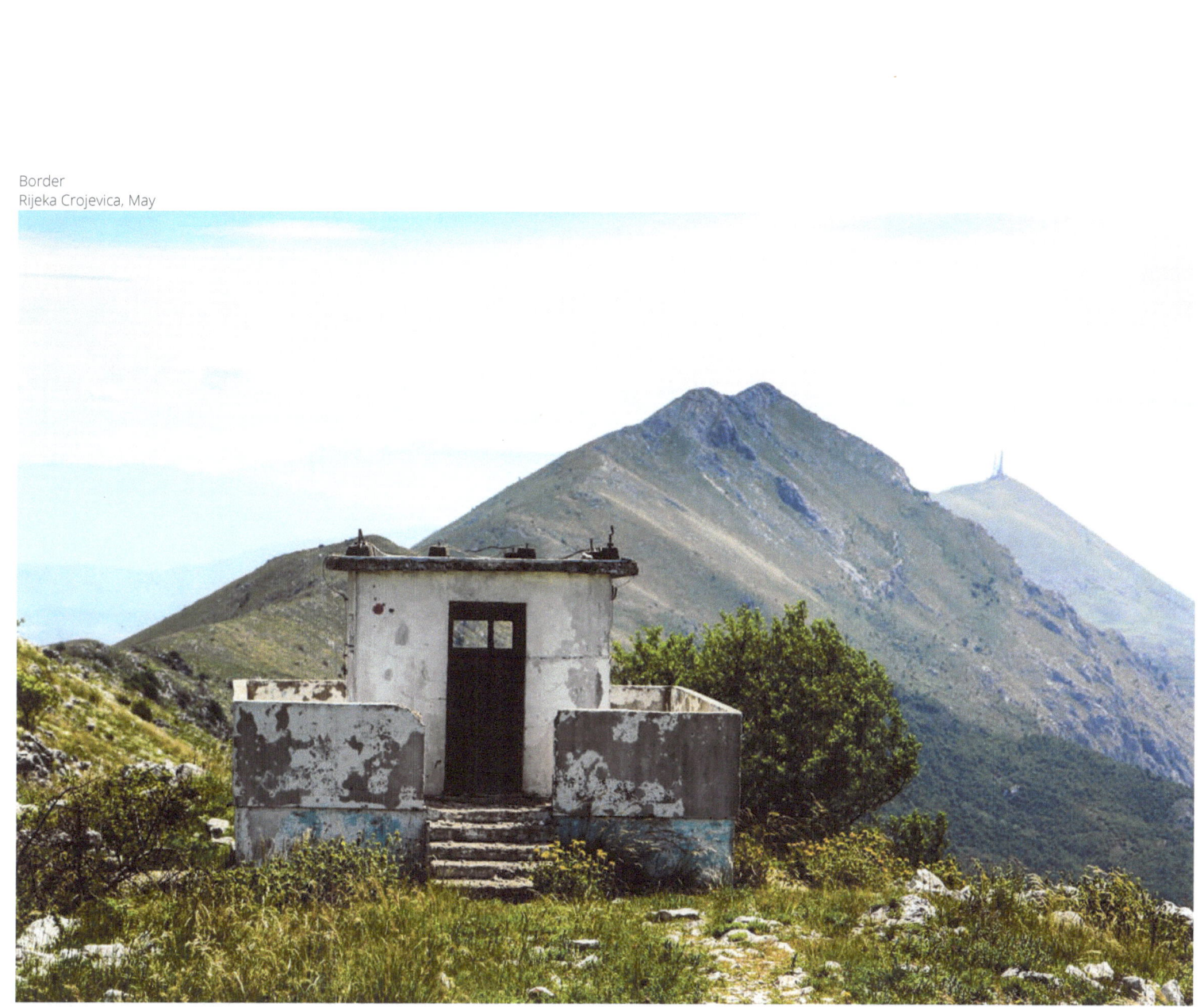

Border
Rijeka Crojevica, May

VRAJNJE SKADARSKO JEZERO RIJEKA
40in14
ASCENT OF ULCINJ RISAN
MONTENEGRO

www.ingramcontent.com/pod-product-compliance
Lightning Source LLC
Chambersburg PA
CBHW050839180526
45159CB00004B/1961